Judge Not! *Is It Legalism to Judge Sin and Error?*

By David Cloud

Judge Not!

Copyright 2006 by David Cloud
ISBN 1-58318-095-8

Published by
Way of Life Literature
P.O. Box 610368, Port Huron, MI 48061
866-295-4143 (toll free) • fbns@wayoflife.org (e-mail)
http://www.wayoflife.org (web site)

Canada:
Bethel Baptist Church, 4212 Campbell St. N., London, Ont. N6P 1A6 • 519-652-2619 (voice) • 519-652-0056 (fax)

Printed in Canada by
Bethel Baptist Print Ministry

Contents

Introduction 4
The Bible Says We Should Not Judge 6
Love is Nonjudgmental and Tolerant 19
Being Strict about Biblical Issues is Legalism 25
Fundamentalists Are Pharisees 33
Jesus Told Us Not to Forbid Others 37
Why Don't You Follow Matthew 18? 40
We Should Heed Gamaliel's Advice 43
We Should Leave the Tares until the Harvest 45
We Should Not Touch the Lord's Anointed 47
If We Don't Stand Together We Will Hang Separately ... 50
The Christian Army Shoots Its Own Wounded 52
God Does Not Look on the External Appearance 55
We Will Be in Heaven Together 57
The Christian Life Should Be Liberty and Fun 58
We Should Be All Things to All Men 68
Denominational Divisions Should Be Erased 70
It is Not Possible to Know That Your Doctrine Is Right ... 77
Loving Jesus Is All that Is Important 80
Fundamentalism Is a Belief in Five Fundamentals 84
We Should Limit Our Message to Broaden Fellowship .. 91
We Should Be Balanced 96

Introduction

Having preached the Word of God for more than three decades I am no stranger to controversy and I am very familiar with the challenges that are given to fundamentalist style preaching.

In 1984 the Lord led me to begin publication of a monthly magazine called *O Timothy*. The title, taken from 1 Timothy 6:20, describes the burden of the magazine, which is urging men in these last days to keep the faith once delivered to the saints and to avoid the error which is on every hand. *"O Timothy, keep that which is committed to thy trust, avoiding profane and vain babblings, and oppositions of science falsely so called."* In 1996 we began the Fundamental Baptist Information Service through which we distribute the same types of articles electronically. Like the magazine, the goal in this particular aspect of our ministry is not devotional but is to assist preachers in the protection of the churches in this apostate hour through doctrinal preaching and carefully documented research.

The response has been overwhelmingly positive by many people and overwhelmingly negative by others.

On the negative side, I can't count the number of times that people have written to challenge and correct me about my stand.

This book contains the chief of these challenges. These are the same challenges that every fundamentalist Bible-believing Christian must learn to deal with. There is no part of the world so remote that the believers there will not be confronted with this thinking.

I trust that my answers to these challenges will be an encouragement and a spiritual protection to many of God's people in these difficult but opportune days.

This material would make a good series of study for Sunday School at the Junior High level or above or for Youth meetings or Bible Schools.

THE BIBLE SAYS WE SHOULD NOT JUDGE

One of the most commonly held myths in contemporary Christianity is the idea that the Bible forbids judging.

The following are some of the key passages that are used to support this doctrine, but when we examine them in context and by comparing Scripture with Scripture, we find that these passages are being greatly abused.

We will begin with the passage that is abused above all others:

MATTHEW 7:1-5 -- Judge not, that ye be not judged. For with what judgment ye judge, ye shall be judged: and with what measure ye mete, it shall be measured to you again. And why beholdest thou the mote that is in thy brother's eye, but considerest not the beam that is in thine own eye? Or how wilt thou say to thy brother, Let me pull out the mote out of thine eye; and, behold, a beam is in thine own eye? Thou hypocrite, first cast out the beam out of thine own eye; and then shalt thou see clearly to cast out the mote out of thy brother's eye."

First, if we examine the context of this passage we see that the Lord Jesus is not condemning all judging; He is condemning hypocritical judging (Mat. 7:5). To forbid something in another person that I allow in my own life is hypocrisy, and it is a great and deep-seated sin among men. For a parent to tell his children not to listen to rock music when he listens to Country-Western music is hypocrisy. To tell my children not to smoke when I smoke or to attend church when I don't attend church, or to be serious about God's will when I am not that serious about His will, or to be kind to others when I am not kind to them or to their mother, or to obey me when I don't obey my husband is hypocrisy. This is the type of thing that Christ was warning about.

This is not to say, though, that Christ forbade judging in general. That He is not condemning all judging is evident from the context. In the same sermon He warned about false prophets.

> "Beware of false prophets, which come to you in sheep's clothing, but inwardly they are ravening wolves. Ye shall know them by their fruits. Do men gather grapes of thorns, or figs of thistles? Even so every good tree bringeth forth good fruit; but a corrupt tree bringeth forth evil fruit" (Mat. 7:15-17).

It is impossible to beware of false prophets without judging doctrine and practice by the God's Word. How can I know who a false prophet is if I do not measure preachers by God's Word?

That Christ is not condemning all judging is also evident by comparing Scripture with Scripture. In other passages we are commanded to judge. The Lord Jesus Himself said we are to judge righteous judgment (Jn. 7:24).

We are to judge sin in the church (1 Cor. 5:3, 12). *"For I verily, as absent in body, but present in spirit, have judged already, as though I were present, concerning him that hath so done this deed, ... For what have I to do to judge them also that are without? do not ye judge them that are within?"*

We are to judge matters between the brethren (1 Cor. 6:5). *"I speak to your shame. Is it so, that there is not a wise man among you? no, not one that shall be able to judge between his brethren?"*

We are to judge preaching (1 Cor. 14:29). *"Let the prophets speak two or three, and let the other judge."*

We are to judge those who preach false gospels, false christs, and false spirits (2 Cor. 11:1-4). *"But I fear, lest by any means, as the serpent beguiled Eve through his subtilty, so your minds should be corrupted from the simplicity that is in Christ. For if he that cometh preacheth another Jesus, whom we have not preached, or if ye receive another spirit, which ye have not received, or another gospel, which ye have not accepted, ye might well bear with him."*

We are to judge the works of darkness (Eph. 5:11). *"And have no fellowship with the unfruitful works of darkness, but rather reprove them."*

We are to judge spirits (1 John 4:1). *"Beloved, believe not every spirit, but try the spirits whether they are of God: because many false prophets are gone out into the world."*

We are even to judge all things (1 Cor. 2:15-16). *"But he that is spiritual judgeth all things, yet he himself is judged of no man. For who hath known the mind of the Lord, that he may instruct him? But we have the mind of Christ."*

The spiritual man does not judge things by his own thinking but by the mind of Christ in the Word of God. He knows that he lives in a fallen world filled with lies and error and spiritual deception and he knows that he has the light of God in the Scripture and he thus judges all things by that.

ROMANS 14:4 -- "Who art thou that judgest another man's servant? to his own master he standeth or falleth. Yea, he shall be holden up: for God is able to make him stand."

This is another passage that is frequently abused by those who have the ecumenical philosophy. It is said that this verse forbids us to expose sin and error and compromise. The verse is also used to support the doctrine that Scripture can be divided into fundamental or essential and non-fundamental or secondary doctrine. One pastor wrote to me and said:

> "Romans 14 is probably the most violated passage by those of us who call ourselves 'fundamentalists' (note that I include myself). We have either skipped over that chapter or given it a sinfully surface interpretation and danced around its powerful mandates for dealing with differences over 'secondary' doctrine within the church. By 'secondary' I do not mean 'unimportant.' I must be 'fully persuaded' about all Scriptural issues, though I must welcome and neither judge nor look down on those who differ on some of them."

To this I gave the following reply:

Romans 14 is an important passage, but it has nothing to do with the idea that there things in Scripture of secondary value in the sense of how we are to deal with them. The two examples given by the apostle are eating meats and keeping holy days. These are matters about which the Bible is silent. There are no divine requirements upon the New Testament Christian concerning these things.

Thus, Romans 14 is discussing how we are to deal with matters NOT CLEARLY TAUGHT IN SCRIPTURE. In matters in which God has not plainly spoken, I am to give liberty.

On the other hand, in matters in which God has plainly spoken, the only liberty is to obey. People use Romans 14:4 to defend many areas of plain disobedience, such as worldly music, long hair on men, immodest dress on women, women preachers, etc. Since the Bible has spoken plainly about these matters, it is a misuse to apply Romans 14:4.

You are missing the mark by a great distance in your understanding of this passage.

1 CORINTHIANS 4:3-5 -- "But with me it is a very small thing that I should be judged of you, or of man's judgment: yea, I judge not mine own self. For I know nothing by myself; yet am I not hereby justified: but he that judgeth me is the Lord. Therefore judge nothing before the time, until the Lord come, who both will bring to light the hidden things of darkness, and will make manifest the counsels of the hearts: and then shall every man have praise of God."

Here is another passage that is misused by those who hold the nonjudgmental philosophy, but Paul is not saying that believers should judge nothing at all and should leave all judgment to God. This would be contrary to many other passages in the same epistle (i.e., 1 Cor. 2:15; 5:3, 12; 6:2-3; 14:29).

He is saying, rather, that believers are not to judge ministers by their own human thinking as to what a minister should be and how he should teach and act, but they are to judge righteous judgment according to God's Word. He is talking about being judged by "man's judgment" (1 Cor. 4:3). It is not required that a minister suit men and bend to their thinking; it is required that he be faithful to God, and this is the only proper standard by which he can be judged.

Paul, under inspiration of the Holy Spirit, is also saying that ultimate and final judgment belongs only to the Lord; therefore, we must be humble and cautious in our judgments in this present time (1 Cor. 4:4-5). Even though we have the Word of God and we are obliged to judge everything on the basis of God's Word, we must not think that we are infallible. We have to walk in the light that we have and live our lives and exercise our ministries on that basis, but our knowledge is very imperfect in this present world.

We can know if a man's teaching is false and we can know enough, therefore, to mark his error and to avoid it, but we do not know the secrets of men's hearts and we do not know all of the things that will be brought to bear and come into play when God judges men in that perfect light of a coming day. Thus we know that all of our judgments in this world are provisional and the final judgment will be given only by God.

JAMES 4:11-12 -- "Speak not evil one of another, brethren. He that speaketh evil of his brother, and judgeth his brother, speaketh evil of the law, and judgeth the law: but if thou judge the law, thou art not a doer of the law, but a judge. There is one lawgiver, who is able to save and to destroy: who art thou that judgest another?"

Like Matthew 7:1, Romans 14:4, and 1 Corinthians 4:5, James 4:11 is frequently misused by the ecumenical crowd to support the false doctrine that Christians are forbidden to judge doctrine and practice. To make these verses teach that Christians can never judge, though, throws the Bible into confusion. There is a right judgment and a wrong judgment. Many verses command us to judge righteous judgment (Luke 12:57; John 7:24; 1 Cor. 2:15). We are to judge preaching (1 Cor. 14:29), sin in the churches (1 Cor. 5:3), issues in the churches (1 Cor. 6:5), sin in our own lives (1 Cor. 11:31), false teachers (Mat. 7:15; Rom. 16:17); spirits (1 John 4:1), etc.

When, then, is James forbidding? The context clarifies the matter.

First, James is referring to evil speaking (Jam. 4:11). Proper judging is to speak the truth in love. The truth is not evil and speaking the truth in love is not evil. The type of judging condemned by James is judging in the sense of tearing down, tale bearing, and slander. It is judging with an evil intent. When one judges sin and error scripturally, it is never with a desire to hurt people. The Pharisees judged Jesus in an evil manner (Jn. 7:52). The false teachers at Galatia and Corinth judged Paul in the same manner, trying to tear him down in the eyes of the churches (2 Cor. 10:10). This is what James forbids, but he is not forbidding the scriptural and compassionate judging of error and of those who promote error.

Second, James is referring to judging in a way that is contrary to the law of God ("*there is one lawgiver,*" Jam. 4:12). This refers to judging others by human standards rather than divine, thus setting oneself up as the lawgiver. The Pharisees did this when they judged Jesus by their traditions (Mat. 15:1-3). On the other hand, when a believer judges things by God's Word in a godly and compassionate manner, he is not exercising his own judgment; he is exercising God's judgment. When, for example, I say that it is wrong for a woman to be a pastor or it is a shame for a man to have long hair or that those who love the world are adulterers, this is not my judgment or law; it is God's (1 Tim. 2:12; 1 Cor. 11:14; Jam. 4:4).

For more on verses misused by the ecumenical movement see the commentaries in *THINGS HARD TO BE UNDERSTOOD* on 1 Sam. 24:4-10; Matt. 18:15-17; Mk. 9:38-40; John 13:35; 17:21; Acts 5:38-39; James 4:11-12. This book if available from Way of Life Literature.

The following additional comments about judging are by the late Franklin G. Huling:

> This question, Is it right to judge? is one that puzzles many sincere Christians. A careful and open-minded study of the Bible makes it clear that concerning certain vital matters, it is not only right but a positive duty to judge. Many do not know that--THE SCRIPTURE COMMANDS TO JUDGE
>
> The Lord Jesus Christ commanded, "Judge righteous judgment" (John 7:24). He told a man, "Thou hast rightly judged" (Luke 7:43). To others, our Lord asked, "Why even of yourselves judge ye not what is right?" (Luke 12:57).
>
> The apostle Paul wrote, "I speak as to wise men; judge ye what I say" (1 Cor. 10:15). Again, Paul declared, "He that is spiritual judgeth all things" (1 Cor. 2:15). It is our positive duty to judge.
>
> ### *False Teachers and False Teaching*
>
> "Beware of false prophets!" (Matthew 7:15) is the warning and command of our Lord. But how could we "beware" and

how could we know they are "false prophets" if we do not judge? And what is the God-given standard by which we are to judge? "To the Law and to the Testimony: if they speak not according to THIS WORD, it is because there is NO LIGHT in them" (Isaiah 8:20). "Ye shall know them by their fruits," Christ said (Mat. 7:16). And in judging the "fruits," we must judge by God's Word, not by what appeals to human reasoning. Many things seem good to human judgment which are false to the Word of God.

The apostle Paul admonished believers, "Now I beseech you, brethren, MARK THEM which cause divisions and offences contrary to the doctrine which ye have learned; and AVOID THEM. For they that are such serve not our Lord Jesus Christ, but their own belly; and by good words and fair speeches deceive the hearts of the simple." (Romans 16:17-18). This apostolic command could not be obeyed were it not right to judge. God wants us to know His Word and then test all teachers and teaching by it. Notice also that it is the false teachers who make the "divisions," and not those who protest against their false teaching. And these deceivers are not serving Christ, as they profess, "but their own belly," or their own "bread and butter as we would put it. We are to "MARK THEM" and "AVOID THEM."

"Come out from among them, and be ye separate, saith the Lord." (2 Cor. 6:17; read also verses 14-18)

"From such turn away" (2 Tim. 3:5). "Withdraw yourselves." (2 Thess. 3:6)

"And have no fellowship with the unfruitful works of darkness, but rather reprove them." (Eph. 5:11)

"ABHOR THAT WHICH IS EVIL; CLEAVE TO THAT WHICH IS GOOD." (Rom. 12:9)

"Prove all things; hold fast that which is good." (1 Thess. 5:21)

It would be impossible to obey these injunctions of God's Word unless it were right to judge. And remember, nothing is "good" in God's sight that is not true to His Word.

The apostle John wrote, "Beloved, believe not every spirit, but try [test, judge] the spirits whether they are of God:

because many false prophets are gone out into the world" (1 John 4:1). Again he wrote, "For many deceivers are entered into the world, who confess not that Jesus Christ is come in the flesh... If there come any unto you, and bring not this doctrine, RECEIVE HIM NOT into your house, neither bid him God speed: For he that biddeth him God speed is partaker of his evil deeds" (2 John 7, 10-11). This Scripture commands us to judge between those who do and those who do not bring the true doctrine of Christ.

Whenever a child of God contributes to a denominational budget that supports Modernist missionaries or teachers, he is guilty before God, according to this Scripture, of bidding them "God speed" in the most effective way possible. And he thereby becomes a "partaker" with them of their "evil deeds" of spreading soul-damning poison. How terrible, but how true! Arouse yourself, child of God. If you are guilty, ask God to forgive you and help you never again to be guilty of the blood of souls for whom Christ died. When we are willing to suffer for Christ, we can readily see the truth of God's Word on this tremendously important matter. "If we suffer, we shall also reign with Him" (2 Tim. 2:12).

The reason Christendom is today honeycombed and paralyzed by Satanic Modernism is because Christians have not obeyed the command of God's Word to judge and put away and separate from false teachers and false teaching when they first appeared in their midst. Physical health is maintained by separation from disease germs. Spiritual health is maintained by separation from germs of false doctrine. The greatest peril of our day is not too much judging, but too little judging of spiritual falsehood. God wants His children to be like the noble Bereans who "searched the Scriptures daily, whether those things were so" (Acts 17:11).

Romans 2:1-3 is also addressed to the religious hypocrite who condemned himself because he was guilty of the same things for which he condemned others. James 4:11-12 refers to an evil spirit of backbiting and fault finding, not to judging whether teachers or teachings agree or disagree with God's Word. The Bible never contradicts itself. To understand one portion of Scripture we must view it in the light of all Scripture. "No prophecy of the Scripture is of any private (isolated) interpretation" (2 Peter 1:20). "Comparing spiritual things (words) with spiritual" (1 Cor. 2:13).

Other Matters to Be Judged

Immoral conduct of professed believers in Christ is to be judged. 1 Corinthians chapter 5 tells a sad story and closes with the apostolic injunction, "Therefore put away from among yourselves that wicked person" (2 Cor. 5:13).

Disputes between Christians concerning "things that pertain to this life" (1 Cor. 6:3) should be judged by a tribunal of fellow Christians instead of going before unbelievers in the civil courts. The whole sixth chapter of 1 Corinthians makes clear God's plan for His people in this regard. And some startling truths are here revealed: First, "the saints shall judge the world." Second, "we shall judge angels" (1 Cor. 6:2- 3). Beloved, are we letting God prepare us for this high place?

We ought to judge ourselves. "Examine yourselves, whether ye be in the faith; prove your own selves" (2 Cor. 13:5). "For if we would judge ourselves, we should not be judged. But when we are judged, we are chastened (child trained) of the Lord, that we should not be condemned with the world" (1 Cor. 11:31-32). What a change and what a blessing it would be if we would judge our own faults as uncharitably as we do the faults of others--and if we would judge the failings of others as charitably as we do our own! And Christians could save themselves much chastening of the Lord if they would judge and confess and cease their disobedience to God. And, O, how much dishonour and lack of fruit would our blessed Lord be spared!

Limitations of Human Judgment

We are not to judge scruples. God forbids our judging our brethren concerning the eating of certain kinds of food, keeping of days, etc. Romans chapter 14; 1 Corinthians 10:23-33; and Colossians 2:16-17 cover this subject.

We are also not to judge motives. See 1 Corinthians 4:1-5. Only God can see into the heart and know the motives that underlie actions.

We are also not to judge who is saved. "The Lord knoweth them that are His" (2 Tim. 2:19). We cannot look into anyone's heart and say whether or not they have accepted the Lord Jesus Christ as their personal Saviour, if they profess that they have. But we had better test ourselves according to 2 Cor. 5:17: "If any man be IN CHRIST, he is a new creature: old things are passed away; behold, all things are become new." If this change has not taken place, our profession is vain.

Elements in Judgment

The New Testament Greek word that is most often translated "judge" or "judgment" is "krino." On the one hand, it means to distinguish, to decide, to determine, to conclude, to try, to think and to call in question. That is what God wants His children to do as to whether preachers, teachers and their teachings are true or false to His Word.

The apostle Paul writes: "And this I pray, that your love may abound yet more and more in knowledge and in all judgment; that ye may approve things that are excellent" (Philippians 1:9-10). A wrong idea of love and lack of knowledge and judgment causes God's people often to approve things that are anything but excellent in God's sight. The epistle to the Hebrews tells us that mature believers, that is, those who are of "full age," are those who by reason of use have their senses exercised to discern both good and evil" (Hebrews 5:14).

On the other hand, the Greek word "krino"--judge or judgment--means to condemn, to sentence, and to punish. This is God's prerogative, for He has said, "Vengeance is Mine, I will repay, saith the Lord" (Rom. 12:19).

Thus Christians are to exercise discernment, but not vengeance.

Guard Against a Wrong Attitude

Christians should watch against the tendency of the flesh to assume a critical and censorious attitude toward those who do not share our opinions about other matters than those which have to do with Bible doctrine and moral conduct. Rather than "pick to pieces" our brethren in

Christ, it is our privilege and duty to do everything we can to encourage their spiritual upbuilding. We ought to love and pray for one another and consider ourselves lest we be tempted.

A Final Word

If you are saved, my reader, let us not forget that "we must all appear before the judgment seat of Christ" (2 Corinthians 5:10). It will be well with those who are studying God's Word, walking in the light of it, living for Christ and the salvation of souls. It will go ill with those who have accepted Christ but who are living for the things of this world.

If you are a mere professor of Christ, or profess nothing, my friend, may I lovingly remind you that "judgment must begin at the house of God; and if it first begin at us, what shall the end be of them that obey not the Gospel?" (1 Peter 4:17). Delay not another moment to ask God for Christ's sake to forgive your sins. Surrender your heart and will to the loving Saviour who died for you. Make Him the Lord of your life. Happy and blessed will you be, now and forever (Franklin G. Huling).

LOVE IS NONJUDGMENTAL AND TOLERANT

When Bible-believing Christians take the Word of God and measure leaders, churches, denominations and movements today by it, ecumenical types invariably charge them with a lack of love. For example, a woman wrote to me and said:

> "You preach separatism. What about unity? You preach about heresy. WHAT ABOUT LOVE? ... From what I have viewed on your website, you hold your views as high as the Bible itself. What you call 'zeal for the Bible' I call arrogance and pride. If you knew the Bible as well as you claim, then I believe you'd live it. The lost will never be reached through such hatred" (Letter from a reader, May 1997).

This lady was upset about my preaching, but instead of explaining my alleged error carefully from the Bible, she charged me with a lack of love, and this, in spite of her own haughty and incredibly judgmental attitude toward me!

To this brainwashed generation, the negative aspects of biblical Christianity are unloving. To carefully test things by the Bible is unkind. To warn of false gospels is uncompassionate. To mark and avoid false teachers is mean-spirited. To preach high and holy standards of Christian living is legalist meanness.

A few years ago, Evangelist Jack Van Impe rejected biblical separatism and went over to the ecumenical philosophy. He said:

> "Let's forget our labels and come together in love, and the pope has called for that. I had 400 verses on love. Till I die I will proclaim nothing but love for all my brothers and sisters in Christ, my Catholic brothers and sisters, Protestant brothers and sisters, Christian Reformed, Lutherans, I don't

care what label you are. By this shall all men know that ye are my disciples if ye have love one to another."

This is the popular view of love, but it is false and dangerous.

Ecumenists Are Confused about the Definition of Love

Love is crucial. The Bible says that without love "I am become as sounding brass, or a tinkling cymbal." The Bible tells us that God is love, and those who know God will reflect His love.

What is love, though? The ecumenical world is confused about its definition. Love must be defined biblically. To human thinking, love is a warm feeling or a romantic thought. "Love," to this ecumenical generation, is broadmindedness and non-judgmental tolerance of any one who claims to know the Lord Jesus Christ.

This is not what the Bible says about love. Consider the following verses of Holy Scripture:

> "Jesus answered and said unto him, IF A MAN LOVE ME, HE WILL KEEP MY WORDS: and my Father will love him, and we will come unto him, and make our abode with him" (John 14:23).

> "And this I pray, that your LOVE MAY ABOUND YET MORE AND MORE IN KNOWLEDGE AND IN ALL JUDGMENT; That ye may approve things that are excellent; that ye may be sincere and without offence till the day of Christ" (Philippians 1:9-10).

> "For THIS IS THE LOVE OF GOD, THAT WE KEEP HIS COMMANDMENTS: and his commandments are not grievous" (1 John 5:3).

> "And we have confidence in the Lord touching you, that ye both do and will do the things which we command you. And the Lord direct your hearts into the love of God, and into the patient waiting for Christ. Now we command you, brethren,

in the name of our Lord Jesus Christ, that ye withdraw yourselves from every brother that walketh disorderly, and not after the tradition which he received of us" (2 Thess. 3:4-6).

Biblical love is obedience to God and His Word. In the last passage cited we see that the love of God is sandwiched between two verses that emphasize obedience to God's commandments, including separation from disobedient brethren!

Love is not a feeling. It is not blissful romanticism. It is not fuzzy toleration of things that are wrong. For a woman to love her husband means she submits to and serves him according to the Bible. For a man to love his wife means he treats her in the way the Bible commands. For children to love their parents means they honor and obey them as the Bible commands. Love is obedience to God's Word.

Love is not an emotion. Emotions are unstable and undependable. Love is not broadmindedness. It is not non-judgmentalism. It is not non-critical tolerance. Biblical love is careful. It is based on the knowledge of God's Word and is associated with the exercise of judgment. It proves all things and approves only those things that are the will of God.

Was the Lord Jesus Christ unloving when He called Peter a devil (Matt. 16:23) or when he publicly condemned the Pharisees (Matthew 23)? Was the apostle Paul unloving when he rebuked Peter for his compromise (Galatians 1)? Was the apostle Paul unloving when he named the name of false teachers and compromisers such as Hymenaeus and Alexander ten different times in the Pastoral Epistles? Was the apostle Paul unloving when he forbade women to preach or to usurp authority over men (1 Tim. 2:12) and required that they keep silent in the churches (1 Cor. 14:34)?

Biblical love does not mean that I ignore things that are wrong and injurious. To love a false teacher does not mean that I turn a blind eye to his error and strive to have unity with him regardless of his doctrine. It means that I obey the Bible and mark and avoid him (Romans 16:17), that I expose his error publicly to protect those who might be led astray by his teaching.

Ecumenists Are Confused about the Direction of Love

Ecumenists are not only confused about the definition of love they are also confused about the direction of love.

THE FIRST DIRECTION OF LOVE MUST BE TOWARD GOD. Ecumenists talk much about love toward man, but what about love toward God? According to the Lord Jesus Christ, what is the greatest commandment?

> "Then one of them, which was a lawyer, asked him a question, tempting him, and saying, Master, which is the great commandment in the law? Jesus said unto him, Thou shalt love the Lord thy God with all thy heart, and with all thy soul, and with all thy mind. This is the first and great commandment. And the second is like unto it, Thou shalt love thy neighbour as thyself" (Matthew 22:35-39).

The first and great commandment is not to love one's neighbor. That is the second commandment. The first and great commandment is to love the Lord God will all of one's heart, soul, and mind.

Ecumenists point their fingers at the Bible-believing

fundamentalist and charge him with a lack of love toward men because he exercises judgment and discipline and separation. What, though, about love for God? The ecumenist tells me that I need to love all the denominations regardless of what doctrine they teach. I reply that I need to love God and His Truth first, and that means that I will obey the Bible, and that means I will measure, mark, and avoid those who are committed to error.

A genuine love for God requires that I care more about His Word and His will than about men and their feelings and opinions and programs.

We agree with Charles Haddon Spurgeon when he said: "On all hands we hear cries for unity in this, and unity in that; but to our mind the main need of this age is not compromise, but conscientiousness. 'First pure, then peaceable.' It is easy to cry 'a confederacy,' but that union which is not based upon the truth of God is rather a conspiracy than a communion. Charity by all means; but honesty also. LOVE, OF COURSE, BUT LOVE TO GOD AS WELL AS LOVE TO MEN, AND LOVE OF TRUTH AS WELL AS LOVE OF UNION. It is exceedingly difficult in these times to preserve one's fidelity before God and one's fraternity among men. Should not the former be preferred to the latter if both cannot be maintained? We think so" (Spurgeon, "The Down Grade - Second Article," *The Sword and the Trowel,* April 1887, Notes, p. 16).

THE DIRECTION OF LOVE NOT ONLY MUST BE TOWARD GOD BUT IT MUST BE TOWARD THOSE WHO ARE IN DANGER. The ecumenical crowd tells me that I need to love the Modernist and the Romanist, etc., but they are practically silent on the subject of love for those who are deceived by the Modernist and the Romanist. We are charged with being unloving, for example, when we expose the fact that John Paul II or Mother Teresa preached a false sacramental gospel. The fact is that we love people enough to warn of false gospels so they will not be led astray to eternal hell.

A shepherd who loves wolves more than the sheep is a confused and wicked shepherd.

In conclusion, we quote from the words of James Henley Thornwell, a staunch Old School Presbyterian preacher who fought against theological modernism in the 19th century. He was the sixth president of South Carolina College (today the University of South Carolina). He was weary with the compromised evangelicals of his day, who said they loved the truth but were soft in their stance and refused to withstand heresy boldly. Note his powerful words and his understanding of true biblical love:

> "To employ soft words and honeyed phrases in discussing questions of everlasting importance; to deal with errors that strike at the foundations of all human hope as if they were harmless and venial mistakes; to bless where God disapproves, and to make apologies where He calls us to stand up like men and assert, though it may be the aptest method of securing popular applause in a sophistical age, is cruelty to man and treachery to Heaven. Those who on such subjects attach more importance to the rules of courtesy than they do to the measures of truth do not defend the citadel, but betray it into the hands of its enemies. Love for Christ, and for the souls for whom He died, will be the exact measure of our zeal in exposing the dangers by which men's souls are ensnared" (quoted in a sermon by George Sayles Bishop, author of *The Doctrines of Grace and Kindred Themes*, 1910).

BEING STRICT ABOUT BIBLICAL ISSUES IS LEGALISM

"Legalism" is a term frequently used to describe Bible-believing Christians who are zealous for pure doctrine and who desire to maintain holy standards of living in this wicked hour. I am called a "legalist" via e-mail at least once a day! Consider a few examples:

> "You, sir, are a legalist that the Pharisees would have been mighty proud of."
>
> "You have a narrow minded legalistic view of Scripture. ... I write contemporary praise music, music that is used in churches in worship of God. It's not for your approval or anyone else no matter what denomination or off the wall sect of a denomination they are."
>
> "Your website makes me cringe. I can understand why this world hates fundamentalist Christians when you write legalistic articles like this. There is no humility in your critiques, only a pharisaical elitism that makes my stomach turn."

The "free thinking" attitude that lies behind the charge of legalism was expressed at a "Christian" rock concert called Greenbelt '83:

> "We don't believe in a fundamentalist approach. We don't set ground rules. Our teaching is non-directive. We want to encourage people to make their own choices."

Those who have this type of mindset label the "old-fashioned" Bible Christian a "legalist," but it is a slanderous and wrongheaded accusation.

What Legalism Is

True legalism has a two-fold definition in the Word of God.

First, legalism is to mix works with grace for salvation (Galatians 1). This is the theme of the epistle of Galatians. Paul warns the churches against turning from the grace of Christ (Gal. 1:6) and emphasizes that salvation is not by works or law-keeping but by the grace of Christ alone.

> "Knowing that a man is not justified by the works of the law, but by the faith of Jesus Christ, even we have believed in Jesus Christ, that we might be justified by the faith of Christ, and not by the works of the law: for by the works of the law shall no flesh be justified" (Gal. 2:16).

> "For as many as are of the works of the law are under the curse: for it is written, Cursed is every one that continueth not in all things which are written in the book of the law to do them. But that no man is justified by the law in the sight of God, it is evident: for, The just shall live by faith" (Gal. 3:10-11).

> "Wherefore the law was our schoolmaster to bring us unto Christ, that we might be justified by faith. But after that faith is come, we are no longer under a schoolmaster" (Gal. 3:24-25).

According to this definition, legalists today are any who add works to the grace of Christ for salvation. The Roman Catholic Church does this. So does the Church of Christ and the Worldwide Church of God and Seventh-day Adventism and many others.

Second, legalism is to add human tradition to the Word of God.

> "Ye hypocrites, well did Esaias prophesy of you, saying, This people draweth nigh unto me with their mouth, and honoureth me with their lips; but their heart is far from me. But in vain they do worship me, teaching for doctrines the commandments of men" (Matt. 15:7-9).

We must be careful never to add our own tradition and teaching to the Word of God. There is one authority for faith and practice, and that is the Bible. Anything that is exalted to a place of authority equal to the Bible is condemned by God.

The Pharisees of old, in committing both of these errors, were true legalists. They rejected the grace of Jesus Christ and taught that the way of salvation was by the keeping of the law and they made their own tradition authoritative over people's lives without a biblical basis.

The Roman Catholic Church also commits both of these errors.

Many others add things to the Word of God today. Christian Science adds Mary Baker Eddy's writings. Seventh-day Adventism adds Ellen G. White's writings. Many Pentecostals and Charismatics add (at least in practice) personal revelations and experience. Some old-time Pentecostals made prohibitions against drinking Coca-Cola and wearing necklaces and exalted these rules to the level of Scripture.

We must be careful when we seek to apply the principles of Scripture to Christian living that we do not fall into this trap today. For example, to set specific standards of modesty for female church workers that are supported by clear Scriptural principles, such as requiring a certain dress length and forbidding shorts, is not legalism, because the Bible requires modesty and forbids nakedness, even defining it as showing the leg and thigh and such (Isa. 47:2-3), and warns about the effect of female dress on the male (Mat. 5:28).

Setting standards can become legalism if the requirements go beyond Scripture. We must be very careful in drawing lines, that our lines are God's and not our own. I have heard of churches that have forbidden men to wear pink shirts, because it is allegedly "feminine," but this is going far out on a limb. The color pink, while vaguely associated with femininity, is not so intricately associated with it that we can make a law about it. Other churches have forbidden beards and facial hair. One mission that supports Central American national pastors has this rule, but it is more than ridiculous; it is legalistic, because not only does the Bible not forbid facial hair on men, it encourages it by the example of Old Testament prophets (Ezr. 9:3) and even Jesus Christ Himself (Isa. 50:6). Beards are mentioned 15 times in the Bible and never in a negative context. Another mission board required that missionaries cannot be interracially married and forbade the missionary couples even to adopt children of another race, but while there are practical issues pertaining to interracial marriages and adoptions, the Bible nowhere strictly forbids this.

Thus, we repeat, we must be very careful in drawing lines, that our lines are God's and not our own.

What Legalism Is Not

Having seen what legalism is, let us now consider what it is not.

In a nutshell, for a Bible preacher to urge God's people to obey the details of God's Word by the grace of Christ cannot be legalism, because this is precisely what God requires. Consider the following Scriptures very carefully.

> "For by grace are ye saved through faith; and that not of yourselves: it is the gift of God: Not of works, lest any man should boast. For we are his workmanship, created in Christ Jesus unto good works, which God hath before ordained that we should walk in them" (Eph. 2:8-10).

Here we see that while the blood-washed saint is saved *by* grace without works, he is saved *unto* good works. The believer obeys God's Word, not in order to be saved but because he has been saved. It therefore cannot be legalism for a preacher to urge God's people to keep the works of God contained in the New Testament faith. I have counted 88 specific commandments in the epistle of Ephesians alone. Consider this one: *"And have no fellowship with the unfruitful works of darkness, but rather reprove them"* (Eph. 5:11). This is a far-reaching requirement. The believer must guard every area of his life, every activity, to make sure that he is not having fellowship with the works of darkness. Not only so, but he is reprove the works of darkness. This is one of the verses that spoke to my heart 32 years ago and convinced me that I had to put rock & roll music out of my Christian life. It is certainly an unfruitful work of darkness, but the requirement does not stop with music. It involves every part of the Christian life, dress, companionship, music, entertainment, literature, relationships with churches and professing believers, you name it. To take such commandments of the New Testament faith seriously and to apply them rigorously cannot, therefore, be "legalism."

> "For the grace of God that bringeth salvation hath appeared to all men, teaching us that, denying ungodliness and worldly lusts, we should live soberly, righteously, and godly, in this present world; looking for that blessed hope, and the glorious appearing of the great God and our Saviour Jesus Christ; Who gave himself for us, that he might redeem us from all iniquity, and purify unto himself a peculiar people, zealous of good works. These things speak, and exhort, and rebuke with all authority. Let no man despise thee" (Titus 2:11-15).

Here, again, we see that the grace of Christ does not teach Christians to live carelessly but to live strictly. The grace of God teaches us to deny ungodliness and worldly lusts, which is a far-reaching obligation. It means that we are to examine every area of our lives and churches in order to root out ungodliness. Again, this involves every aspect of the Christian life, dress, companionship, music, entertainment, literature, you name it.

And notice in Titus 2:15, that the Spirit of God concludes this passage about avoiding ungodliness with the following exhortation to preachers: "*These things speak, and exhort, and rebuke with all authority. Let no man despise thee.*" The preacher has a solemn obligation before God to speak, exhort, and rebuke on the basis of these passages. It cannot, therefore, be any sort of "legalism" if a preacher takes this obligation seriously and applies this teaching to every area of life, speaking, exhorting, and rebuking about ungodliness and worldly lusts in the area of music and dress, companionship, entertainment, etc.

> "I charge thee therefore before God, and the Lord Jesus Christ, who shall judge the quick and the dead at his appearing and his kingdom; preach the word; be instant in season, out of season; reprove, rebuke, exhort with all longsuffering and doctrine" (2 Tim. 4:1-2).

Here we see a similar obligation to the one in Titus 2:15. The preacher has a solemn responsibility before God for his preaching and he will give an account to Jesus Christ. He is to preach the Word. What part of it? All of it! He is not only to read the Word verbatim; he is to preach it and to apply it to the people's everyday lives. He is to reprove, rebuke, and exhort. He is to make sure that the Word of God gets down to where the people live, to apply it to every aspect of their individual lives, their family lives, their employment, their service for Christ, their companionships, their entertainment, their dress, their music, you name it. The Word of God speaks to every area of life, and the preacher is obligated to follow it wherever it leads. This is definitely not "legalism."

> "Teaching them to observe all things whatsoever I have commanded you: and, lo, I am with you alway, even unto the end of the world. Amen" (Matt. 28:20).

This is part of the obligation of Christ's Great Commission. Those who believe the gospel and are baptized are to be taught to keep ALL things that He has commanded. This is another far-reaching requirement. It means that the churches are to be concerned about all of the New Testament faith and not just some part of it that happens to be popular at the moment, and they are to train their people to keep all of it. The churches are obligated, therefore, to teach separation from the world, separation from false teaching, rejection of heretics, church discipline, the reality of eternal hell, repentance, denial of self, everything; they must teach the popular things and the unpopular. To take Christ's commandment seriously and to seek to be faithful to the whole New Testament faith cannot, therefore, be "legalism."

Strict obedience to God's Word by Christ's grace is the way of liberty, not bondage.

> "Then said Jesus to those Jews which believed on him, If ye continue in my word, then are ye my disciples indeed; and ye shall know the truth, and the truth shall make you free" (John 8:31-32).

The love of God is to obey His commandments. *"For*

this is the love of God, that we keep his commandments: and his commandments are not grievous" (1 John 5:3).

The believer does not keep the Word of God in his own power and strength or to his own glory. He keeps it by the power of the indwelling Christ and to His glory. "*I am crucified with Christ: nevertheless I live; yet not I, but Christ liveth in me: and the life which I now live in the flesh I live by the faith of the Son of God, who loved me, and gave himself for me*" (Gal. 2:20).

FUNDAMENTALISTS ARE PHARISEES

Christians who stand for the details of the Word of God and preach against that which they believe to be error, who exalt biblical morality and preach against immorality, and who have strong biblical convictions are often labeled "Pharisees." Many of the Promise Keepers supporters who have written to me to rebuke me for reproving their movement, call me a Pharisee. Consider a couple of examples:

> "Rev. Cloud says 'Our sole authority is the Bible.' No one who participated in the Council of Carthage in 387 which settled for all time the canon of the NT would agree with Rev. Cloud on this issue. ... Such arrogance! ... I take it then, that you're the only one going to heaven. It's going to be awfully lonely there. Such arrogance! ... Such arrogance! ... I wonder what makes Mr. Cloud so sure he's right and everybody else is wrong? Look at the Pharisees, Mr. Cloud, and then look in the mirror!"

> "You're the best example I think I've ever seen of the Pharisee who sits at the front of the synagogue giving thanks for not being a sinner like everyone else."

To label a Bible-believing Christian who has zeal to obey God's Word a Pharisee is a slander, because the error of Phariseeism was not their zeal to obey the Scripture. They had no such zeal. They were zealous, rather, to make up their own religious system and to rule over the people.

It is important to note that Jesus Christ did NOT rebuke the Pharisees for their zeal in obeying the details of the law. He said to them: *"Woe unto you, scribes and Pharisees, hypocrites! for ye pay tithe of mint and anise and cummin, and have omitted the weightier matters of the law, judgment, mercy, and faith: these ought ye to have done, and not to leave the other undone*" (Matt. 23:23).

Christ did not rebuke the Pharisees for paying attention to the less weighty things in the law. He rebuked them for focusing on the lesser matters to the neglect of the weightier ones.

The Bible-believing fundamentalists that I know do not neglect the weightier matters of the New Testament faith. They aim, rather, to follow Paul's example and to give heed to "the whole counsel of God" (Acts 20:27). They preach the virgin birth, blood atonement, resurrection, and ascension of Christ and justification by grace and the Trinity and the personality of the Holy Spirit and the other "weightier" matters of the faith, but they also preach church discipline (1 Cor. 5) and the restrictions upon the woman's ministry (1 Tim. 2:12; 1 Cor. 14:34) and due order among men and women, which even touches on their hair styles (1 Cor. 11:1-16) and other things that are less weighty than salvation by grace and the deity of Jesus Christ.

We can see what Phariseeism is by examining what Christ rebuked for:

(1) Phariseism is supplanting the Word of God with man-made tradition and thereby making the Word of God of none effect. "*Ye hypocrites, well did Esaias prophesy of you, saying, This people draweth nigh unto me with their mouth, and honoureth me with their lips; but their heart is far from me. But in vain they do worship me, teaching for doctrines the commandments of men*" (Matt. 15:7-9).

(2) Phariseeism is rejecting Jesus Christ. *"Then was brought unto him one possessed with a devil, blind, and dumb: and he healed him, insomuch that the blind and dumb both spake and saw. And all the people were amazed, and said, Is not this the son of David? But when the Pharisees heard it, they said, This fellow doth not cast out devils, but by Beelzebub the prince of the devils"* (Matt. 12:22-24).

(3) Phariseeism is perverting the Gospel of the free grace of Christ into a work's salvation. *"Woe unto you, scribes and Pharisees, hypocrites! for ye compass sea and land to make one proselyte, and when he is made, ye make him twofold more the child of hell than yourselves"* (Matt. 23:15).

(4) Phariseeism is self-righteousness. *"And he spake this parable unto certain which trusted in themselves that they were righteous, and despised others: Two men went up into the temple to pray; the one a Pharisee, and the other a publican. The Pharisee stood and prayed thus with himself, God, I thank thee, that I am not as other men are, extortioners, unjust, adulterers, or even as this publican. I fast twice in the week, I give tithes of all that I possess"* (Lk. 18:9-12).

(5) Phariseeism is gross hypocrisy. *"In the mean time, when there were gathered together an innumerable multitude of people, insomuch that they trode one upon another, he began to say unto his disciples first of all, Beware ye of the leaven of the Pharisees, which is hypocrisy"* (Lk. 12:1).

The Pharisees were at the forefront of the crucifixion of Jesus Christ and of the persecution of the early Christians.

It is a great error to label a Christ-loving, Bible-honoring, grace gospel-preaching, self-debasing, peace-loving Christian a Pharisee.

I can't speak for all Bible-believing fundamentalists and fundamental Baptists, but I can speak for myself; and I have no confidence in my "righteousness." I know that I have no righteousness apart from Jesus Christ. I look down upon no man, for I know that any spiritual victory I have enjoyed and any blessing in my life is only because of the grace of Christ. When I attempt to expose false teaching and sin, I am not looking down upon other men; I am simply striving to obey the Word of God.

The modern Pharisee would be more akin to the Roman Catholic priest with his sacramental gospel and his traditions exalted to the place of Scripture and his long history of persecuting the saints. The ecumenical crowd doesn't call Catholic priests Pharisees, though. They don't seem to be concerned about all of the souls who have been led astray by these contemporary Pharisees.

The only men they seem to be concerned about are those dreadful old fundamentalists with their strong Bible convictions and their refusal to smile at error. Oh, those dreadful old fundamentalist Pharisees!

JESUS TOLD US NOT TO FORBID OTHERS

Mark 9:38-40 - "And John answered him, saying, Master, we saw one casting out devils in thy name, and he followeth not us: and we forbad him, because he followeth not us. But Jesus said, Forbid him not: for there is no man which shall do a miracle in my name, that can lightly speak evil of me. For he that is not against us is on our part."

Luke 9:49-50 - "And John answered and said, Master, we saw one casting out devils in thy name; and we forbad him, because he followeth not with us. And Jesus said unto him, Forbid him not: for he that is not against us is for us."

These passages are frequently abused by those who promote ecumenical fellowship and unity. When a preacher exposes the compromise and error of some Christian leader or movement, they protest that this is not God's will and they cite these verses as evidence. They say, "Don't you know that Christ said you should not forbid another professing Christian who is doing works in His name."

We know that this is a misuse of Scripture because the Bible does not contradict itself. If the Lord Jesus Christ was saying in these passages that it is wrong to judge and expose error, He would be contradicting His own Word. Many other Scriptures describe the preacher's responsibility to judge doctrine and to warn publicly of error and compromise. See, for example, Matthew 7:15; 16:6-12; 24:4,5; Romans 16:17; 1 Cor. 14:29; Galatians 1:8,9; Philippians 3:2; Colossians 2:8; 2 Thess. 3:14; 1 Timothy 4:1-6; 2 Timothy 2:16-18; Titus 1:9-11; 1 John 4:1; 2 John 8-11; Jude 3; Revelation 2:6, 14, 15.

We know, therefore, that whatever the Lord Jesus Christ is saying in the aforementioned passages, He is *not* saying that it is wrong to mark and expose the error and compromise of Christian leaders.

In truth Christ was forbidding the disciples to exercise ecclesiastical control over other men who claim to follow Him. He was warning against that natural impulse to control others. He was not saying that we cannot *reprove* another Christian; He was saying that we cannot *forbid* another Christian. These are completely different things.

The apostles had great authority to establish the first churches and to complete the canon of Scripture, but they did not have unlimited authority. They were not popes. Their objective was not to establish the kingdom of God by force. They could not bear the sword against those who refused to follow them. They could not exercise physical force against those they considered their enemies. They could not imprison them or beat them or confiscate their property or kill them or otherwise seek to "forbid" them to preach.

The Roman Catholic Church ignored this warning and claimed authority over all Christians. Rome attempted to forbid all men to serve Christ unless they served Him after the Roman Catholic fashion.

The preacher that exposes error is not trying to forbid other men to preach the gospel or to serve Christ. He is not exercising authority over anyone or persecuting anyone. He is merely doing what the Word of God requires; he is measuring men and movements by the Scripture.

When I warn of dangers I see in Billy Graham's ecumenical crusades, for example, and I warn about how he has turned converts over to the Roman Catholic

Church, I am not forbidding him to preach the gospel nor am I trying to exercise any type of authority over him. I can praise the Lord for every soul that is genuinely saved through the Billy Graham Evangelistic Crusade or any other movement. I do not try to stop them with force or governmental authority or human deception. The weapons of our warfare are not carnal.

This does not mean, though, that I am going to ignore error. I must reprove heresy and compromise and earnestly contend for the faith once delivered to the saints, and to do so is not contrary to what Christ forbade.

WHY DON'T YOU FOLLOW MATTHEW 18?

From time to time I am asked if I follow the guidelines of Matthew 18 before I publish a report. For example, when I published a gentle warning about some of the newer *Patch the Pirate* music tapes, I received three or four notes from readers asking if I had first approached Majesty Music. Following is one of these:

> "I am writing to ask if you follow the principles of Matthew 18 when writing about a brother in Christ? Have you gone to Brother Hamilton about your concerns alone, before writing your critique? Did you find no satisfaction and take another brother in Christ with you? I recognize these are steps to be followed in a local church context, but it seems prudent and wise and God honoring to follow similar steps when dealing with brothers and sisters from other churches."

Another man gave the same sort of challenge in regard to my warnings about Chuck Swindoll:

> "I have read your article on Chuck Swindoll. It is not our job to judge our fellow man. If you have concerns with Swindoll and his teachings then your job is to confront him personally, speak to and with him, find out where he is coming from. If you still believe he is wrong then bring it before your eldership and let them confront. Then, and only then, if there is still no change, you bring it before the congregation, and then you leave it and him in God's hands."

In reality, Matthew 18 gives instructions for dealing with personal problems between Christians. It does not address how to deal with public teachings and actions by Christian leaders. The apostle Paul, in the Pastoral Epistles, mentioned the names of compromisers and false teachers TEN times, warning Timothy about them. Those letters were not intended merely for Timothy and

Titus. They were a part of the canon of Scripture and were a public record. Paul's motive was not to injure those men. There was nothing malicious in his warnings. His motive was to protect godly preachers and sound churches.

Matthew 18 deals with personal trespasses between members of an assembly. Consider exactly what the passage says:

> "Moreover if thy brother SHALL TRESPASS AGAINST THEE, go and tell him his fault between thee and him alone: if he shall hear thee, thou hast gained thy brother. But if he will not hear thee, then take with thee one or two more, that in the mouth of two or three witnesses every word may be established. And if he shall neglect to hear them, TELL IT UNTO THE CHURCH: but if he neglect to hear the church, let him be unto thee as a heathen man and a publican" (Matthew 18:15-17).

Majesty Music has not trespassed against me individually. Chuck Swindoll has not trespassed against me. That is not the issue here, and it would be impossible to follow Matthew 18 in this situation. Even if I were to attempt to follow the first part of the passage in such a context, it would be impossible to follow the last part. I have no way to take this issue "unto the church." I am not a member of these men's churches. Their churches have no authority over me, and I have no business with them (and I am sure they would ignore any attempt I might make to bring accusations against these men). Similarly, these men are not members of my church, so they have no business with it and it has no authority over him.

To attempt to follow Matthew 18 in such matters would be confusion.

Chuck Swindoll, etc. has published materials and

distributed them widely to individuals and churches across the land. I am merely analyzing their published works in obedience to the Word of God. Material that is distributed publicly should be analyzed publicly.

Following are some of the Scriptures that give me authority for this practice:

> "Prove all things; hold fast that which is good" (1 Thessalonians 5:21).
>
> "Preach the word; be instant in season, out of season; reprove, rebuke, exhort with all longsuffering and doctrine" (2 Timothy 4:2).
>
> "And have no fellowship with the unfruitful works of darkness, but rather reprove them" (Ephesians 5:11).
>
> "These things speak, and exhort, and rebuke with all authority. Let no man despise thee" (Titus 2:15).
>
> "Beloved, when I gave all diligence to write unto you of the common salvation, it was needful for me to write unto you, and exhort you that ye should earnestly contend for the faith which was once delivered unto the saints" (Jude 3).

By the way, my personal correspondence with Majesty Music was completely ignored, even though I approached them humbly as a friend who has advertised their music for many years (and continues to do so) without charge. Human nature does not like to be corrected, and the bigger the ministry the more inured it thinks itself to be from criticism.

WE SHOULD HEED GAMALIEL'S ADVICE

> Acts 5:38-39 - "And now I say unto you, Refrain from these men, and let them alone: for if this counsel or this work be of men, it will come to nought: But if it be of God, ye cannot overthrow it; lest haply ye be found even to fight against God."

Gamaliel was an unconverted Pharisee and God used him to deliver Peter and John from death, but he said a foolish thing which many Christians quote as gospel truth.

Gamaliel advised the Jewish rulers not to kill Peter and John who had been preaching Christ contrary to Jewish law.

Some use this to support the idea that it is none of our business to rebuke sin or to expose false theology. We should leave that to God. Like Gamaliel, they say if the work be of God, it will grow; if it is not, it will fail, so just leave it alone.

To cite Gamaliel as an authority, though, is to follow the philosophy of unsaved man. The Bible only quotes what Gamaliel said; it does not approve his statement.

It is not true that if a work be not of God, "it will come to nought." The Jehovah's Witnesses movement has not come to nought even though it denies Christ's deity and salvation by grace. The same is true for Buddhism and Hinduism and Mohammedism and Romanism and Spiritism and Mormonism.

It is a foolish and unscriptural principle to say that we are to leave false things alone.

Timothy was commanded, "Them that sin rebuke before all, that others also may fear" (1 Tim. 5:20). Paul instructed Titus to deal with false teachers: "Wherefore rebuke them sharply, that they may be sound in the faith" (Titus 1:13). Ephesians 5:11 says we are to reprove the unfruitful works of darkness. Jude 3 says we "should earnestly contend for the faith which was once delivered unto the saints."

"Some follow Gamaliel, but it would be far better if they would follow the Bible" (John R. Rice, *Ecumenical Excuses for Unequal Yokes*).

WE SHOULD LEAVE THE TARES UNTIL THE HARVEST

> "Another parable put he forth unto them, saying, The kingdom of heaven is likened unto a man which sowed good seed in his field: But while men slept, his enemy came and sowed tares among the wheat, and went his way. But when the blade was sprung up, and brought forth fruit, then appeared the tares also. So the servants of the householder came and said unto him, Sir, didst not thou sow good seed in thy field? from whence then hath it tares? He said unto them, An enemy hath done this. The servants said unto him, Wilt thou then that we go and gather them up? But he said, Nay; lest while ye gather up the tares, ye root up also the wheat with them. Let both grow together until the harvest: and in the time of harvest I will say to the reapers, Gather ye together first the tares, and bind them in bundles to burn them: but gather the wheat into my barn" (Matthew 13:24-30).

This parable is misused by many who do not like the practice of separation. They say, "Christ taught us to ignore the tares until the time of harvest when the angels will sort things out. It is not our job today to root out the tares from the churches and to separate the tares from the wheat."

The parable is not referring to the churches, though. Christ plainly said "the field is the world" (verse 38).

The parable teaches that the final separation of the saved from the unsaved can only be accomplished by God at the coming of Christ. The parable forbids the type of thing that was practiced by the Roman Catholic Church during the Middle Ages, when Rome joined hands with the secular powers to enforce their laws against all men. Those deemed "heretics" were persecuted and even burned to death. This is condemned by Christ's parable and by many other passages of the New Testament. It is not the church's business to discipline the world.

It *is* the church's business, though, to discipline its own members. Heretics, after the first and second admonition, are to be rejected (Titus 3:10-11).

It also the business of the Christian to separate from false teachers (Romans 16:17; 2 Timothy 3:5; 2 John 10-11).

The following is by the late Franklin G. Huling:

> "The 'Wheat and the Tares' parable of Matthew 13:24-30, 36-43, is also much misunderstood. First of all, our Lord is talking about the world, not His Church--'the field is the world.' He goes on to say that 'the good seed are the children of the Kingdom; but the tares are the children of the wicked one' (Matthew 13:38). They are the two groups in the world, children of God--those who have received Christ (John 1:12), and the children of the devil--those who reject Christ (John 8:44).
>
> "When any of the 'children of the wicked one' get into the professed church of Christ, as they have always done, a definite procedure for God's children is set forth in His Word. First, it is their duty to tell them that they have 'neither part nor lot' in Christ (see Acts 8:21-23 and context). If the children of the devil do not leave voluntarily, as is generally the case, God's children are commanded to 'purge out' these unbelievers (1 Cor. 5:7). But God's people have disobeyed His Word about this, and so unbelievers have gotten into control, as is now the case in most denominations.
>
> "Therefore, those who purpose to be true to Christ and His Word are commanded to 'come out from among them, and be ye separate, saith the Lord' (2 Cor. 6:17), regardless of property or any other considerations. When we obey God's Word, we can trust Him to take care of all the consequences of our obedience."

WE SHOULD NOT TOUCH THE LORD'S ANOINTED

The following is by Dennis Costella, Director of the Fundamental Evangelistic Association, Los Osos, California. Used by permission.

Clever "one-liners" and biblical phrases lifted out of context are heard on every hand today. More often than not, they tend to encourage what God has forbidden, or to discourage what God's Word has commanded. As Bible believers, we must exercise great care when we speak to an issue. Our response must be with the correct application of Truth, and not with a commonly used idiom that unwarily pops into the mind and rolls easily off the tongue.

Consider the expression "touch not the Lord's anointed." Time and again we hear this cry parroted as a counter to those who attempt to alert the unsuspecting of the dangerous, unbiblical teachings of a particular ministry. As a result, key religious figures fall into a category that is apparently safe from scriptural examination; since their ministries influence millions, they MUST be God's anointed--don't you dare "touch" them!

If you give a warning about doctrinal inconsistencies within the programs headed by men such as Billy Graham, Bill Bright, Jimmy Swaggart or even the pope, you can be sure that in the estimation of many, the moment the word of caution was uttered, you became guilty of "touching the Lord's anointed"! This indictment sounds ominous to say the least, but the question still remains, "What does God's Word have to say about this?" That's what really matters.

A look at the actual context from which this phrase is lifted provides clear-cut proof that scriptural reproof and rebuke does NOT constitute "touching God's anointed" at all.

David's warning against touching the Lord's anointed was giving in reference to harming the king. See 1 Samuel 24:6, 10; 26:11, 16, 23.

In spite of this, God made sure that Saul was forced to face up to his compromise. The ministry of the king of Israel was judged according to the Lord's commandments, and no man today is exempt from this same kind of biblical scrutiny.

David refused to slay King Saul with the sword, even though in doing so he would rid himself of his arch enemy, and also clear the way for his own ascent to the throne of Israel (1 Sam. 24:1-15). God, not David, would remove Saul in His time and in His way (1 Sam. 26:8-10).

But some say there is a "secondary application" found in this text which would also bar ANY negative comment about another's far-reaching ministry, for this, too, would constitute "speaking against" one of God's servants and is, in essence, "touching God's anointed." Is this a viable, secondary application? Absolutely not!

Samuel certainly "touched God's anointed," if by that you mean speaking out against his disobedience (1 Sam. 15:20). God told Saul to "smite Amalek, and utterly destroy all that they have, and spare them not..." (1 Sam. 15:3). But under a pretext of pious intention, he "spared the best of the sheep and of the oxen, to sacrifice unto the Lord" (v. 15). Partial obedience. Samuel said it was tantamount to witchcraft and idolatry! TO OBEY is better than sacrifice!!!

Saul had a very visible testimony that affected all of God's people. When he failed to minister according to the absolute standard, God's faithful prophet was commanded to cry out against the error. Take his life-- no, rebuke his sins--yes! Let's get straight what the Bible forbids in this account, and what it demands. Scriptural reproof and rebuke of a disobedient brother is not "touching God's anointed." It is compliance with God's order. [This study on the Lord's anointed is by Dennis Costella, Director of the Fundamental Evangelistic Association, Los Osos, California. Used by permission.]

IF WE DON'T STAND TOGETHER WE WILL HANG SEPARATELY

The following is by Dennis Costella, Director of the Fundamental Evangelistic Association, Los Osos, California. Used by permission.

The expression "we will either stand together or we will hang separately" is often advanced by the new-evangelical, and sad to say even by some supposed fundamentalists, in an effort to justify unbiblical fellowships while opposing common enemies. Fundamentalists today join in common cause, not only with compromised brethren, but also with liberals and outright cultists to fight immorality, abortion or other evils. But has God suspended His guidelines for separation from whatever is contrary to doctrinal purity for the sake of added political or theological clout? No!

The fact remains, God will bless the testimony of a separated witness and will perform His will in and through it, rather than condone an alliance built upon compromise.

The notion that a visible unity wields more influence with the powers of this world is humanistic reasoning, not divine revelation. Stand true! Stand alone if need be! In so doing, you need never fear being "hung" by anyone as long as your sole confidence is in God, and not in the strategy of men.

God's Word still declares that the source of power in opposing the evil of our day comes from absolute dependence on the arm of God, not on the concerted efforts of men. The biblical doctrine of separation is based on the premise that the holiness of God will never allow for the joining together of that which is true to the Word, and what is contrary to the Word in a common cause, regardless of how righteous or needful it might appear to be.

The end does not justify the means in Christian ministry.

> "Be ye not unequally yoked together with unbelievers: for what fellowship hath righteousness with unrighteousness? and what communion hath light with darkness? And what concord hath Christ with Belial? or what part hath he that believeth with an infidel? And what agreement hath the temple of God with idols? for ye are the temple of the living God; as God hath said, I will dwell in them, and walk in them; and I will be their God, and they shall be my people. Wherefore come out from among them, and be ye separate, saith the Lord, and touch not the unclean thing; and I will receive you, And will be a Father unto you, and ye shall be my sons and daughters, saith the Lord Almighty" (2 Corinthians 6:14-18).

[The previous study on standing together or hanging separation is by Dennis Costella, Director of the Fundamental Evangelistic Association, Los Osos, California. Used by permission.]

THE CHRISTIAN ARMY IS THE ONLY ONE THAT SHOOTS ITS OWN WOUNDED

Through the years, I have frequently heard the accusation that preachers who give specific warnings about Christian leaders are guilty of "shooting their own wounded." Recently I received the following e-mail that charges me with doing this:

> "I grew up in Murfreesboro, TN and was and am still associated with the Sword of the Lord and the Bill Rice Ranch. I hated it then and still do when another Christian brother bashes another Christian brother over things instead of preaching and trying to win souls to Christ. It is said that the Christian Army is the only army that stabs its wounded and kills off its own. I have to say it is very true. I am also a Marine, and we were taught to pick up those who are wounded and even dead, not leave them to die or to be mutilated by the enemy. We as Christians do just the opposite many times."

What does "shooting their own wounded" mean? If it means that Christians sometimes fail to be patient with the weak, it is true. If it means that Christians sometimes criticize a fellow believer instead of trying to help him, it is all too true; and we need to be reminded often that God is not pleased with such things.

If, on the other hand, it means that it is wrong for a preacher to identify and warn of those who are teaching error, it is nonsense.

In my ministry of warning, I have not injured any of the Lord's wounded and I have never shot anyone in any sense whatsoever. To charge me with doing so is to confuse reproof, correction, and discernment with assault. I was in the army and I understand the military, and what I am doing has absolutely nothing to do with shooting one's own wounded.

The leaders that I warn about are not wounded; they are willfully and steadfastly committed to error and are leading others into that error. (By the way, they don't mind "shooting" back!)

The Lord Jesus Christ taught His people to beware of false prophets (Matt. 7:15). When a preacher obeys this command and attempts to mark and warn of false teachers, is he "shooting the wounded"? No, but those he warns about and those who are sympathetic to them will charge him with doing so.

In 1 and 2 Timothy, the apostle Paul names the names of false teachers and compromisers 10 different times and warns about them (1 Tim. 1:20; 2 Tim. 1:15; 2:17; 3:8; 4:10, 14). All of the men that Paul warned about claimed to be Christians and it is likely that they felt that Paul was being unfair and mean-spirited in singling them out. When Paul warned Timothy that Demas had abandoned him because he loved this present world (2 Tim. 4:10), Paul was not shooting at a wounded Demas; but worldly Demas and his associates might have changed him with this.

The Lord has commanded the assemblies to exercise discipline toward unrepentant church members who are committed to gross sin and error (1 Corinthians 5; Titus 3:10, 11). Is that shooting the wounded? It is oftentimes considered so by those who are the objects of the discipline and by those who are sympathetic to them; but proper church discipline, though severe, is not destructive. It has a three-fold goal of glorifying Christ in His church, purifying the congregation, and bringing the sinner to repentance.

Those who are disobedient and compromising commonly mistake correction for persecution and reproof for assault.

Evangelist Chuck Cofty is a highly decorated United States Marine officer who has survived many shocking battlefield experiences. Since he understands these matters extremely well, I asked him to reply to this man's accusation. Following is his statement:

> "Dear Brother Cloud: To my knowledge you have not struck anyone violently or injured them by striking. He no doubt is referring to the many truths that appear in your writings as well as the writings of others concerning contemporary theology that you quote. Some, perhaps even this man, are so timid that when truth is revealed they find it difficult to accept and wind up tolerating error or ignorance for fear of offending someone. When men are named, places identified and error revealed, it is upsetting to those that are 'moderate' in their position. Brother Cloud, it is true that marines never leave their dead on the field of battle and will on occasion render aid to a wounded enemy. This however is situational and conditional as we will not allow such aid to encumber us, slow us down, deter us from our mission or jeopardize our success. Our desire to serve our dear Lord must be the same. I personally think that this dear brother's analogy is poor and his accusation unfounded."

Dennis Costella, Director of the Fundamental Evangelistic Association, Los Osos, California, adds: "It's sad when biblical exhortation is equated to 'taking pot shots' at another. God's Word tells the faithful servant to '... reprove, rebuke, exhort with all longsuffering and doctrine' (2 Tim. 4:20). With respect to the disobedient brother we are to '... note that man, and have no company with him... yet count him not as an enemy, but admonish him as a brother' (2 Thess. 3:6,14-15). This is not 'shooting the wounded'; it is employing God's methodology for healing the breach caused by straying from the divine Standard!"

GOD DOES NOT LOOK ON THE EXTERNAL APPEARANCE

> "And it came to pass, when they were come, that he looked on Eliab, and said, Surely the LORD'S anointed is before him. But the LORD said unto Samuel, Look not on his countenance, or on the height of his stature; because I have refused him: for the LORD seeth not as man seeth; for man looketh on the outward appearance, but the LORD looketh on the heart" (1 Samuel 16:6-7).

Those who follow the contemporary movements in Christianity often use this verse as a proof text for their doctrine that the external is unimportant. The Christian rock crowd uses it to defend their habit of patterning their appearance and demeanor after secular rockers. "God looks on the heart," they say, "so don't worry about the outward appearance."

But 1 Samuel 16:6-7 has nothing whatsoever to do with dress. It has to do with one's natural looks, with stature and countenance. Samuel thought God had chosen Eliab, David's oldest brother (1 Sam. 17:13, 28), to be the king because of his appearance, but God told him that He does not select men for service based on how they look but on the condition of their hearts. This is still the basis upon which God calls men today. It doesn't matter how tall a man is or how naturally distinguished he might look or how much of a natural leader he appears to be. Physical characteristics are not the standard.

To use this verse to support the idea that it does not matter what a Christian wears or how he looks is to rip it out of its context and make it to say something that it does not even hint at. If God cares nothing about how His people dress, the Bible would say nothing about it, but in fact it does.

In the Old Testament the Mosaic Law forbade men and women to dress like the opposite sex. "The woman shall not wear that which pertaineth unto a man, neither shall a man put on a woman's garment: for all that do so are abomination unto the LORD thy God" (Deut. 22:5). In the very beginning, after man sinned, God rejected his partial fig-leave covering and clothed him with coats (Gen. 3:7, 21). Bible forbids any sort of nakedness and defines it even as uncovering the leg and baring the thigh (Isa. 47:2-3).

The New Testament says Christian women are to dress modestly (1 Tim. 2:9). It says women should have long hair and men short hair (1 Cor. 11). The Lord Jesus warned that men are influenced by how women are dressed, because they can commit adultery in their hearts just by looking upon them (Mat. 5:28).

Thus, it does matter how a Christian dresses.

SINCE WE WILL BE IN HEAVEN TOGETHER WE SHOULD GET ALONG ON EARTH

Many have written to challenge me with this thought. They say, "You spend your time warning about this Christian and that Christian; don't you realize that we will all be together in heaven? Why can't we then get along on earth?"

The simple answer is that we will be perfect in heaven, but that certainly is not true on earth. In heaven there will be no false teaching or sin or worldliness or compromise. There will be nothing to reprove.

Meanwhile, we aren't in heaven yet. That is the sweet by and by, and we yearn to be there, but in the mean time we live in the nasty now and now.

And in the nasty now and now God has commanded us to earnestly contend for the faith and to reprove the works of darkness and to do many other things that we won't be doing in heaven.

THE CHRISTIAN LIFE SHOULD BE LIBERTY AND FUN

People, in the name of "freedom," frequently leave good fundamentalist Bible-believing churches to join one of the looser, easy-going congregations that abound in these apostate end-times. Commonly, they are lackadaisical about church attendance, putting more emphasis upon personal and family relaxation and recreation, upon sports and the great outdoors and an endless variety of activities unconnected with God's service or wearing only the thinnest veneer of some type of Christian service to salve the conscience. They exchange their feminine dresses for pants and shorts and other immodest attire, even joining the near-naked crowd at the beaches. They trade the old hymns of the faith for the jazzy charismatic "praise" music and for Christian rock. They develop a more careless attitude toward doctrine, emphasizing, instead, "love" and "unity," fellowshipping with anyone who "loves Jesus" regardless of whether they are committed to sound doctrine. Their ecumenical sympathies increase dramatically, as does their aversion to biblical separation.

When asked about the change, they testify: "I feel more *liberty* now, more *love*; I am having *fun*; I am glad to be free of *legalism*; I don't hear *criticism* at my church; no one *judges* what others do."

Through the years, I have witnessed with sorrow a number of Christian friends who were captured in this fleshly trap.

These are confused about the nature of Biblical

Christianity. Consider the following Bible preachers. Would a person who focuses on liberty and fun be comfortable under such preaching?

James

"Ye adulterers and adulteresses, know ye not that the friendship of the world is enmity with God? whosoever therefore will be a friend of the world is the enemy of God" (James 4:4).

John the Disciple

"Love not the world, neither the things that are in the world. If any man love the world, the love of the Father is not in him. For all that is in the world, the lust of the flesh, and the lust of the eyes, and the pride of life, is not of the Father, but is of the world. And the world passeth away, and the lust thereof: but he that doeth the will of God abideth for ever" (1 John 2:15-17).

John the Baptist

"But when he saw many of the Pharisees and Sadducees come to his baptism, he said unto them, O generation of vipers, who hath warned you to flee from the wrath to come? Bring forth therefore fruits meet for repentance: And think not to say within yourselves, We have Abraham to our father: for I say unto you, that God is able of these stones to raise up children unto Abraham. And now also the ax is laid unto the root of the trees: therefore every tree which bringeth not forth good fruit is hewn down, and cast into the fire" (Matt. 3:7-10).

Peter

"As obedient children, not fashioning yourselves according to the former lusts in your ignorance: But as he which hath called you is holy, so be ye holy in all manner of conversation; Because it is written, Be ye holy; for I am holy. And if ye call on the Father, who without respect of persons judgeth according to every man's work, pass the time of your sojourning here in fear" (1 Peter 1:14-17).

Paul

"Let no man deceive you with vain words: for because of these things cometh the wrath of God upon the children of disobedience. Be not ye therefore partakers with them. For ye were sometimes darkness, but now are ye light in the Lord: walk as children of light: (For the fruit of the Spirit is in all goodness and righteousness and truth;) Proving what is acceptable unto the Lord. And have no fellowship with the unfruitful works of darkness, but rather reprove them" (Ephesians 5:6-11).

"For the grace of God that bringeth salvation hath appeared to all men, Teaching us that, denying ungodliness and worldly lusts, we should live soberly, righteously, and godly, in this present world; Looking for that blessed hope, and the glorious appearing of the great God and our Saviour Jesus Christ; Who gave himself for us, that he might redeem us from all iniquity, and purify unto himself a peculiar people, zealous of good works" (Titus 2:11-14).

These men do not sound like contemporary liberty-fun sort of guys, to me. They preached liberty from eternal destruction through the blood of Christ, but they did not preach liberty to live as one pleases.

The term "liberty" is used in these two different ways in the book of Galatians. Paul refers to the believer's liberty from a works gospel (Gal. 2:4), but he warns of using Christian liberty as an "occasion for the flesh." "For, brethren, ye have been called unto liberty; ONLY USE NOT LIBERTY FOR AN OCCASION TO THE FLESH, but by love serve one another" (Gal. 5:13). The Christian has no liberty to walk in any type of unholiness, no liberty for moral looseness, no liberty to serve the world.

To the liberty-fun Christian, his personal freedom is the chief issue in the decisions he makes about daily living. To the Bible-believing Christian, God's pleasure and the edification of God's people and the salvation of the unsaved is the chief issue.

There is no emphasis upon "fun" in the Bible. The emphasis is upon unquestioning obedience, extreme spiritual caution, and spotless separation from the world. The Christian is depicted as a soldier in a war (2 Tim. 2:3-4). A good soldier is not motivated to exercise his "rights" to have liberty and fun; he is motivated to make every necessary sacrifice and to obey every command that he might win the conflict. Referring to the Christian life, an old song wisely says, "It's a battlefield, brother, not a recreation room; a fight and not a game."

The previously quoted Bible preachers sound like the old-fashioned Bible-believing men of God of past generations who railed against sin and called God's people to holiness and separation from this wicked world. The average contemporary Christian today is not comfortable under this type of preaching. If these holy men of old were to stand before them and preach what we have recorded in our Bibles, no doubt they would be labeled judgmental, fun-hating legalists.

Sadly, those who are crying for liberty and fun are described in 2 Timothy 4:3-4.

> "For the time will come when they will not endure sound doctrine; but after their own lusts shall they heap to themselves teachers, having itching ears; And they shall turn away their ears from the truth, and shall be turned unto fables."

They search out teachers who will preach a positive Christianity and who will encourage their idolatry of "fun" and their yearnings for carnal "liberty."

1 Corinthians 6:12 and 10:23

Someone might reply, "But Brother Cloud, aren't you forgetting 1 Corinthians 6:12 and 10:23?" No, I am not forgetting them. Consider the verses in their context:

> 1 Corinthians 6:12-13 -- "All things are lawful unto me, but all things are not expedient: all things are lawful for me, but I will not be brought under the power of any. Meats for the belly, and the belly for meats: but God shall destroy both it and them. Now the body is not for fornication, but for the Lord; and the Lord for the body."

> 1 Corinthians 10:23-24 -- "All things are lawful for me, but all things are not expedient: all things are lawful for me, but all things edify not. Let no man seek his own, but every man another's wealth."

These verses are frequently misused today by those who desire liberty to fulfill their carnal desires. These would have us believe that the apostle Paul is saying the Christian has liberty to wear immodest clothing and watch indecent movies and romp near naked at the beach and listen to wicked rock music and to fellowship with anyone who says he "loves Jesus" regardless of his doctrinal beliefs, etc.

Is that what the Holy Spirit through Paul meant by the statement "all things are lawful unto me"? By no means! Obviously there are limitations on the Christian's liberty. The New Testament Scriptures, in fact, put great limits upon our "liberty." We are not free to commit fornication (1 Cor. 6:16-18; 1 Thess. 4:3-6), nor to be involved in any sort of uncleanness (1 Thess. 4:7), nor to fellowship with the unfruitful works of darkness (Eph. 5:11), nor to be drunk with wine (Eph. 5:18), nor to allow any corrupt communication to proceed out of our mouths (Eph. 4:29), nor to allow any filthiness of the flesh or spirit (2 Cor. 7:1), nor to be involved in anything that has even the appearance of evil (1 Thess. 5:22), nor to love the things that are in the world (1 John 2:15-17), nor to befriend the world (James 4:4), nor to dress immodestly (1 Tim. 2:9), etc.

What, then, did the apostle mean? He meant that the Christian has been set free by the blood of Christ, free from the wages of sin, free from the condemnation of the law, free from the ceremonies of the Mosaic covenant, *but not free to sin, and not free to do anything that is not expedient or edifying*.

Paul explains himself perfectly in both passages. In 1 Corinthians 6:12-13, he uses the example of eating meat. In 1 Corinthians 8:1-13 and 10:23-28 he uses the example of eating things that have been offered to idols. In all such things like that, the Christian is free, because these are matters in which the Bible is silent. There are no dietary restrictions for the New Testament Christian as there were under the Mosaic Law. We do not have to fear idols; we know they are nothing. This is the type of thing Paul is referring to in 1 Corinthians, if we would only allow him to explain himself in the very context rather than attempt to put some strange meaning upon his words that would fill the Bible with contradiction.

Paul addresses exactly the same thing in Romans chapter 14. The Christian is free from laws about eating and keeping holy days (Rom. 14:2-6). We are not to judge one another in these matters, because these are matters on which the Bible is silent in this dispensation. This does not mean we are not to judge *anything* and that we are free to do whatever we please. When the Bible has spoken on any issue, our only liberty is to obey.

The contemporary philosophy is contrary to the entire tenor of the New Testament writings and is an appalling perversion of these passages.

Four Tests for Christian Activities

In the two passages in Corinthians Paul gives four tests to determine whether the Christian should allow a certain thing in his life:

(1) Does it bring me under its power?

(2) Is it expedient?

(3) Does it edify?

(4) Does it help or hinder my fellow man or does it cause him to stumble?

Again, these are tests that are applied not to sinful things which already are forbidden to the Christian, but to things the Bible does not specifically address.

The sincere application of these tests to things commonly allowed in the world of contemporary Christianity would put a quick stop to many practices. Rock music does bring people under its power; it does not spiritually edify; it is influenced by demons (a simple study of the history of rock music will confirm this) and is not therefore expedient for the Christian who is instructed to be sober and vigilant against the wiles of the devil; it appeals to the flesh which the Christian is supposed to crucify.

Immodest clothing, such as shorts and bathing suits, *does* hinder our fellow man by putting before him a temptation to sin in his thought life; it does not edify those who see us clothed in such a fashion; it does cause others to stumble.

Ecumenical relationships between those who believe sound New Testament doctrine and those who do not, hinders my fellow man and causes him to stumble by confusing him about what is true and what is false Christianity, by giving him the impression that doctrine is not important. Such relationships are not edifying because they weaken the believer's spiritual discernment and zeal for the faith once delivered to the saints.

The Bible says we have liberty in Christ, liberty from eternal condemnation, liberty to serve God and to enjoy our unspeakably wonderful salvation in Christ. It does not say, though, that we have *liberty to do whatever we please with our lives or to do anything that is not expedient or edifying*.

The apostle Paul had such a low view of "personal liberty" that he was willing to forego the eating of meat for the rest of his life if he thought that such eating would offend his brother or cause his brother to stumble in any way (1 Cor. 8:13). He did not have the idea that he was in this world to live as he pleased.

Contrast this apostolic view of Christian liberty with that which is so popular today. Those who are consumed with their "liberty" will not forego even highly questionable things for the sake of glorifying Christ and edifying their fellow man. When confronted with such things, they become puffed up and lash out against a straw man they call "legalism."

A Slippery Slope

Dear friends, beware of this trap. It is a slippery slope. Once you have begun to fight for your "liberty," **where do you stop?** If you accept the lie that the very concept of drawing a line for Christian standards is "legalistic," that the emphasis of the Christian life should be upon "liberty," **you suddenly have no boundaries. We have seen repeatedly that there is no stopping. Those who enter this path are on a backward, downward slide.**

At first the women fight for the "liberty" to wear loose pants, but soon they are wearing tight pants. They fight for the "liberty" to wear loose-fitting shorts, but soon they are wearing shorter and tighter ones. They want the liberty to miss some church services, but soon they are missing many. They want the liberty to bob their hair, but soon they style it like a man's. They want the liberty to listen to jazzy praise music, but soon they are addicted to contemporary hard rock. They want the liberty to watch some questionable videos, but soon they are watching R-rated ones and beyond. They want the liberty to fellowship with those who are "evangelical," but soon they are fellowshipping even with those who have a false gospel. Or at least they become sympathetic with and defensive of those who are doing such things.

You do not lose anything by holding the strictest line of Christian standards in this present evil world, but you have much to lose if you loosen those standards.

One thing those who let down their standards often lose is their children, to the world.

> "For, brethren, ye have been called unto liberty; ONLY USE NOT LIBERTY FOR AN OCCASION TO THE FLESH, but by love serve one another" (Galatians 5:13).
>
> "As free, and NOT USING YOUR LIBERTY FOR A CLOAK OF MALICIOUSNESS, but as the servants of God" (1 Peter 2:16).

"While they promise them liberty, they themselves are the servants of corruption: for of whom a man is overcome, of the same is he brought in bondage" (2 Peter 2:19)

WE SHOULD BE ALL THINGS TO ALL MEN

In 1 Corinthians 9:22 Paul said: "To the weak became I as weak, that I might gain the weak: I am made all things to all men, that I might by all means save some."

If this is isolated from the rest of Scripture one could assume that Paul was willing to do anything to reach the lost, including adopting their lifestyle. This is a doctrine that is popular among the "rock & roll Christian" crowd today.

However, when one examines the context and compares Scripture with Scripture, we find that Paul did not mean this.

In 1 Cor. 9:21, for example, he says, *"To them that are without law, as without law, (being not without law to God, but under the law to Christ,) that I might gain them that are without law."*

Thus, he explains that he is always under the law to Christ and he is never free to do things that would be contrary to the Scripture. For example, Paul would not adopt long hair in order to reach the heathen, because Christ's law says long hair is a shame (1 Cor. 11:14).

And in 1 Cor. 9:27 he says, *"But I keep under my body, and bring it into subjection: lest that by any means, when I have preached to others, I myself should be a castaway."*

Thus, Paul was always strict and he did not allow anything that would result in spiritual carelessness and the possibility of becoming spiritually shipwreck. He always kept his body in subjection.

In Galatians 5:13 he says, *"For, brethren, ye have been called unto liberty; only use not liberty for an occasion to the flesh, but by love serve one another."*

Thus, Paul's liberty was not the liberty to serve the flesh in any sense. One of the first fleshly things that God dealt with me about after I was saved in the summer of 1973 was rock & roll. In my estimation, it is one of the most powerful fleshly things in society today. Steven Tyler of Aerosmith testified that rock music "is the strongest drug in the world" (*Rock Beat*, Spring 1987, p. 23), and LSD guru Timothy Leary added his amen to that, admitting, "I've been STONED ON THE MUSIC many times." My own experience with rock & roll before I was converted agrees with these testimonies, and I am confident that those who believe rock & roll can be used properly in the service of a holy God are deceived.

Paul also taught that believers are to "abstain from all appearance of evil" (1 Thess. 5:22). This is the strictest form of separation, and Paul would not have done anything contrary to this in his own life and ministry.

Paul is definitely not providing a defense for the contemporary Christian rock & roll philosophy and there is no possibility that he would have adopted such a lifestyle. Jeremiah warned, "Learn not the way of the heathen" (Jer. 10:2), and Paul would certainly not have tattooed himself and grown his hair long and adopted pagan music and dress and posture in order to reach the pagans.

DENOMINATIONAL DIVISIONS SHOULD BE ERASED

One of the theme songs of the ecumenical movement is "God is destroying denominational lines." This, of course, is one of the goals of the Promise Keepers movement. They are breaking down the walls between denominations. At the Promise Keepers Clergy Conference in Atlanta in February 1996, the more than 39,000 pastors attending were urged to commit themselves to the "Atlanta Covenant." One of the points of this seven-part document urges pastors to reach beyond racial and DENOMINATIONAL barriers." Promise Keepers founder Bill McCartney made the following statement at this conference: "Contention between denominations has gone on long enough. If the church ever stood together, Almighty God would have his way."

This is a gross error that ignores the apostasy of our time and also the reason for such divisions.

The "Breaking Down Denominational Walls" Mentality Ignores Apostasy

This thinking sounds good to this itching-ear generation (2 Tim. 4:3-4), but it ignores the wretchedly apostate condition of a great many of the denominations.

Respected evangelical leader Harold Lindsell gave this testimony in regard to the mainline denominations:

> "It is not unfair to allege that among denominations like Episcopal, United Methodist, United Presbyterian, United Church of Christ, the Lutheran Church in America, and the Presbyterian Church U.S.A. THERE IS NOT A SINGLE THEOLOGICAL SEMINARY THAT TAKES A STAND IN

FAVOR OF BIBLICAL INFALLIBILITY. AND THERE IS NOT A SINGLE SEMINARY WHERE THERE ARE NOT FACULTY MEMBERS WHO DISAVOW ONE OR MORE OF THE MAJOR TEACHINGS OF THE CHRISTIAN FAITH" (Harold Lindsell, *Battle for the Bible*, Zondervan, 1976, pp. 145-146.)

"Apostasy" refers to falling away from the true New Testament faith, and it is not a figment of a fundamentalist's imagination; it is a Bible doctrine. The New Testament describes two separate streams of "Christianity" operating side by side throughout the church age.

First, there are sound apostolic churches, against which the gates of hell shall not prevail. They will be persecuted, hated, despised, yet they will continue holding to the New Testament faith century after century until Christ's return. The Lord Jesus promised His faithful ones: "Lo, I am with you alway, EVEN TO THE END OF THE WORLD" (Matthew 28:20).

Second, there are apostate churches, which will increase in number and grow worse and worse as the centuries pass. Consider the following Scriptures:

> "For I know this, that after my departing shall grievous wolves enter in among you, not sparing the flock. Also of your own selves shall men arise, speaking perverse things, to draw away disciples after them" (Acts 20:29-30).

> "Now the Spirit speaketh expressly, that in the latter times some shall depart from the faith, giving heed to seducing spirits, and doctrines of devils; Speaking lies in hypocrisy; having their conscience seared with a hot iron; Forbidding to marry, and commanding to abstain from meats, which God hath created to be received with thanksgiving of them which believe and know the truth" (1 Timothy 4:1-3).

> "But evil men and seducers shall wax worse and worse, deceiving, and being deceived" (2 Timothy 3:13).

"For the time will come when they will not endure sound doctrine; but after their own lusts shall they heap to themselves teachers, having itching ears. And they shall turn away their ears from the truth, and shall be turned unto fables" (2 Timothy 4:3-4).

"But there were false prophets also among the people, even as there shall be false teachers among you, who privily shall bring in damnable heresies, even denying the Lord that bought them, and bring upon themselves swift destruction. And many shall follow their pernicious ways; by reason of whom the way of truth shall be evil spoken of. And through covetousness shall they with feigned words make merchandise of you: whose judgment now of a long time lingereth not, and their damnation slumbereth not" (2 Peter. 2:1-3).

"Beloved, believe not every spirit, but try the spirits whether they are of God: because many false prophets are gone out into the world" (1 John 4:1).

"Beloved, when I gave all diligence to write unto you of the common salvation, it was needful for me to write unto you, and exhort you that ye should earnestly contend for the faith which was once delivered unto the saints. For there are certain men crept in unawares, who were before of old ordained to this condemnation, ungodly men, turning the grace of our God into lasciviousness, and denying the only Lord God, and our Lord Jesus Christ" (Jude 3-4).

The parables of Christ in Matthew 13 depict the course of this present "church age" and describe a progression of apostasy. The parable of the leaven in Mat. 13:33, for example, describes a woman putting leaven into three measures of meal, *"till the whole was leavened."* Leaven in Scripture stands for sin and error (1 Cor. 5:6; Gal. 5:9). Thus the parable tells us that the error that was introduced by false teachers even during the days of the apostles will gradually increase through the centuries until the entire religious system is leavened. The ultimate fulfillment of this is in Revelation 17.

Another passage that teaches the same truth is 2 Thessalonians 2:7-8. *"For the mystery of iniquity doth already work: only he who now letteth will let, until he be taken out of the way. And then shall that Wicked be revealed, whom the Lord shall consume with the spirit of his mouth, and shall destroy with the brightness of his coming."*

The "mystery of iniquity" is that program of evil whereby the devil is attempting to corrupt the churches of Jesus Christ by sowing tares and apostasy. It is associated with "Mystery Babylon the Great" in Revelation 17. In the days of the apostles the "mystery of iniquity" was already working, and it will culminate in the promotion of the man of sin, the Wicked One, the Antichrist, who will assume the throne of this world for a brief span. We are told that the culmination of this will not occur until just prior to the return of Christ, because the Wicked One will be destroyed "with the brightness of his coming."

We see the direct fulfillment of these prophecies in the Christian world today. It is clearly witnessed in heretical bodies such as the Roman Catholic Church and the liberal Protestant and Baptist denominations associated with the World Council of Churches. It is also evident in the ecumenical movement, which is calling for unity in diversity at the expense of biblical truth and which is breaking down the walls of separation between truth and error.

Modernism and apostasy has permeated the mainline Christian denominations. Any call, therefore, to breach denominational barriers today, is a call to yoke truth together with error and is an open denial of the biblical doctrine of separation.

The "Breaking Down Denominational Walls" Mentality Ignores the Importance of Bible Doctrine

The push to "break down denominational walls" also ignores the fact that denominational differences are largely doctrinal differences, and the Bible highly exalts doctrine. The Scripture was given for doctrine (2 Tim. 3:16).

While some divisions between Christians are manmade and unnecessary, many others, most, in fact, are doctrinal.

Why, for example, is an Episcopal church different from an independent Baptist church? They have different doctrine. One teaches baptismal regeneration; the other, that baptism is symbolic only. One baptizes infants; the other practices believer's baptism. One sprinkles; the other immerses. One has a priesthood; the other has pastors and deacons. One has a hierarchical church structure; the other practices the autonomy of the assembly. One interprets prophecy literally and is looking for the imminent return of Jesus Christ; the other interprets prophecy symbolically and is working to establish the kingdom of God on earth. One allows its leaders and members to hold every sort of heresy and immorality; the other (generally speaking) practices discipline and separation.

What is the difference between an Assemblies of God congregation and an independent Baptist church? Again, it is doctrine. One believes the baptism of the Holy Spirit is subsequent to salvation and is something the believer must seek and that its manifestation is tongues-speaking; the other believes the baptism of the

Holy Spirit occurred at Pentecost and that every believer is baptized by the Holy Spirit when he is saved. One believes the sign gifts are operative today; the other believes the sign gifts were given to the apostles and ceased with their passing. One believes the Holy Spirit "slays" people; the other, that "spirit slaying" is unscriptural. One believes the gift of tongues is operative today; the other, that the gift of tongues had a temporary purpose that ceased in the first century. One believes salvation can be lost; the other, that salvation is eternally secure. One believes ecumenical unity is the work of the Holy Spirit; the other believes ecumenical unity is the work of the devil.

Those who call for the removal of denominational divisions are ignoring these serious doctrinal differences. Any Bible doctrine worth believing is worth fighting for.

When Paul wrote to Timothy to instruct him in the work of the Lord, he did not tell him to "lighten up" and to ignore doctrinal differences. He solemnly instructed him to remain absolutely steadfast in the apostolic doctrine and not to allow ANY other doctrine to be taught.

> "As I besought thee to abide still at Ephesus, when I went into Macedonia, that thou mightest charge some that they teach NO OTHER DOCTRINE" (1 Timothy 1:3).
>
> "And the things that thou hast heard of me among many witnesses, THE SAME commit thou to faithful men, who shall be able to teach others also" (2 Timothy 2:2).

The believer is instructed to "earnestly contend for the faith which was once delivered unto the saints" (Jude 3). There is not a hint here or anywhere else in Scripture that some part of the Christian faith is of such little importance that it is to be disregarded for the same of a broader unity.

The ecumenical attitude toward doctrine and the push to "break down denominational" walls is not Scriptural and must be resisted.

Those who have the most to lose from the ecumenical call to dissolve denominational walls are those whose doctrine is based upon the Word of God.

IT IS NOT POSSIBLE TO KNOW WHETHER YOUR DOCTRINE IS RIGHT

Doctrine is often downplayed today in favor of ecumenical unity. The following statement by pop singer Pat Boone, who is a Charismatic Christian, typifies the popular attitude toward doctrine:

> "Doctrine divides, experience unites. We don't all have our doctrine all completely correct, but God doesn't judge us on our understanding of doctrine" (Pat Boone, August 17, 2001, cited from *Calvary Contender*, Sept. 15, 2001).

Boone claims that since allegedly don't have our doctrine completely correct and God doesn't judge us about doctrine, let's just focus on unity. This idea is widely held. Many have written to me and said in effect, "Who do you think you are? Do you believe that your doctrine is right and everyone else's is wrong? You can't know that."

But this is not what the Bible says.

The Bible says the believer *CAN* know sound doctrine.

In 2 Timothy 2:15 the believer is commanded to rightly divide the Word of God.

> "Study to shew thyself approved unto God, a workman that needeth not to be ashamed, rightly dividing the word of truth."

To rightly divide the Word of God means to interpret it properly and to know its doctrine correctly. Why would God require a Christian to rightly divide the Word of Truth unless He would give him the ability to do that? This verse indicates that God will hold the Christian accountable for this task, because only the one who rightly divides the word of truth is approved.

The Bible tells us exactly how to know the correct doctrine.

1. <u>We know sound doctrine through obedience</u>. The Lord Jesus Christ gave the following promise in regard to knowing sound doctrine: *"If any man will do his will, he shall know of the doctrine, whether it be of God, or whether I speak of myself"* (John 7:17). To know sound doctrine one must be willing to obey the truth. If a man is open to the truth and willing to obey God, the Lord will give him wisdom so that he will be able to discern sound doctrine from false. In Proverbs 1:23, God says, *"Turn you at my reproof: behold, I will pour out my spirit unto you, I will make known my words unto you."* God has promised to make His truth known to those who submit themselves to Him.

2. <u>We know sound doctrine through continuing in God's Word</u>. The Lord Jesus made another promise in regard to knowing the truth, as follows: *"Then said Jesus to those Jews which believed on him, If ye continue in my word, then are ye my disciples indeed; and ye shall know the truth, and the truth shall make you free"* (John 8:31-32). This precious promise clearly states that a child of God can know the truth. To do so, he must continue in God's Word. This means he must read it, study it, memorize it, love it, and seek to obey it.

3. <u>We know sound doctrine through the Holy Spirit</u>. 1 Jn. 2:20-21 says, *"But ye have an unction from the Holy One, and ye know all things. I have not written unto you because ye know not the truth, but because ye know it,*

and that no lie is of the truth." Verse 27 says further, "*But the anointing which ye have received of him abideth in you, and ye need not that any man teach you: but as the same anointing teacheth you of all things, and is truth, and is no lie, and even as it hath taught you, ye shall abide in him.*" Thus the Scriptures plainly state that the believer has the Holy Spirit to teach him and he can thereby know the truth.

If the ecumenical philosophy is correct and a believer cannot be certain of sound doctrine, the commandments and promises of God make no sense.

LOVING JESUS IS ALL THAT IS IMPORTANT

The ecumenical movements of our day claim that all those who "love Jesus" and "believe the gospel" should be able to fellowship and work together, but there is a serious problem with this philosophy. It ignores the fact that there are many false christs and false gospels. Almost 2,000 years ago the apostle Paul warned of this problem:

> "But I fear, lest by any means, as the serpent beguiled Eve through his subtlety, so your minds should be corrupted from the simplicity that is in Christ. For if he that cometh preacheth another Jesus, whom we have not preached, or if ye receive another spirit, which ye have not received, or another gospel, which ye have not accepted, ye might well bear with him" (2 Corinthians 11:3,4).

The Corinthian church was careless and carnal and tolerant of error, and Paul was afraid that if false teachers came to them with "another spirit" and preached "another Jesus" or "another gospel," they would put up with them instead of separating from them.

This is a perfect description of those who are involved with the modern ecumenical movement. Instead of testing everything carefully by the Word of God and plainly exposing false christs and false gospels, they glory in their tolerance and "unity in diversity."

A perfect example of this is the March for Jesus rallies which are held annually and which seek to draw together all professing Christians for a united "testimony for Jesus." Marty Klein, the national coordinator for March for Jesus in Canada in 1996, testified that Mormons were welcome to participate.

Alan Sharpe of Ottawa wrote to Klein on May 2, 1996, and asked, "I am interested in the March for Jesus. Can a devout Mormon who loves Jesus march in the march?"

Klein replied: "ALL are welcome to join us. However, we make it clear that this is a march FOR Jesus. It is not a protest--we are not promoting anything, but a person (Jesus) and we will not allow Christians or otherwise to parade their various causes."

Sharpe wrote again on May 11 and asked for confirmation about Mormons participating in March for Jesus. He said: "If I want to call myself a good Mormon then I must believe what the elders teach, that Lucifer is Jesus' brother, and that Jesus was a polygamist, and that His wives included Mary and Martha (the sisters of Lazarus) and Mary Magdalene. This is all orthodox Mormonism. ... Can a devout Mormon who believes these things but loves Jesus and wants to praise him still march in the March for Jesus?"

Klein replied: "NO ONE KNOWS what is going on in one's heart except God and that person. Jesus told us if we believe on him and keep his commandments--if we have a personal encounter with him and KNOW we are indwelt by his Spirit then we ARE his children. IN ANY EVENT, I STILL MAINTAIN ----- ALL are welcome to join us. However, we make it clear that this is a march FOR Jesus. It is not a protest--we are not promoting anything, but a person (Jesus) and we will not allow Christians or otherwise to parade their various causes." (emphasis in the original)

This statement demonstrates an incredible ignorance of

the Word of God. Consider some of the false christs that are in the world today:

1. The Wafer Jesus who is worshipped in the Roman Catholic mass.

2. The Mormon Jesus who was a polygamist.

3. The Modernist Jesus who was not born of a virgin.

4. The Unitarian Jesus who was not God.

5. The Universalist Jesus who will not send anyone to Hell.

6. The Prosperity Jesus who was wealthy.

7. The Laughing Jesus who "slays" people with his spirit and causes them to laugh uncontrollably and to stagger like drunk men.

8. The Self-esteem Jesus who never called man a sinner and who came merely to build up his self image.

9. The Revolutionary Jesus who was the founder of Liberation Theology.

These are just a few of the false christs in the world today. Beware of those who refuse to expose false christs and false gospels. It is impossible to love the true Jesus without hating the false ones. Those who claim that God has called them to preach only a positive message and not to enter into theological controversy are greatly deceived.

> "For many deceivers are entered into the world, who confess not that Jesus Christ is come in the flesh. This is a deceiver and an antichrist. Look to yourselves, that we lose not those things which we have wrought, but that we receive a full reward. WHOSOEVER TRANSGRESSETH, AND ABIDETH NOT IN THE DOCTRINE OF CHRIST, HATH NOT GOD. He that abideth in the doctrine of Christ, he hath both the Father and the Son" (2 John 7-9).

"Beloved, when I gave all diligence to write unto you of the common salvation, it was needful for me to write unto you, and exhort YOU THAT YE SHOULD EARNESTLY CONTEND FOR THE FAITH which was once delivered unto the saints" (Jude 3).

FUNDAMENTALISM IS A BELIEF IN THE FIVE FUNDAMENTALS

Some have concocted a position that Fundamentalism historically was not separatistic, but was merely a belief in "the five fundamentals." That this is a serious perversion of history is clear from the following facts.

We must note at the outset of these considerations that Fundamentalism has never been a monolithic movement. It has taken many different forms. There have always been those who have worn the Fundamentalist label who have shied away from the heat of the battle, who have refused to obey the Word of God and separate from error. Describing Fundamentalism is a little like the ant describing the elephant. There are many aspects to Fundamentalism and describing the movement depends somewhat upon one's perspective. Even so, to claim that Fundamentalism was NOT characterized by militancy for truth, to claim that fighting and separating have NOT been a significant aspect of historic Fundamentalism, is to fly in the face of history.

1. THAT HISTORIC FUNDAMENTALISM WAS MORE THAN THE AFFIRMATION OF "THE FIVE FUNDAMENTALS" IS ADMITTED BY ITS HISTORIANS.

George Marsden gives this overview: "By the 1930s, then it became painfully clear that reform from within could not prevent the spread of modernism in major northern denominations, MORE AND MORE FUNDAMENTALISTS BEGAN TO MAKE SEPARATION FROM AMERICA'S MAJOR DENOMINATIONS AN

ARTICLE OF FAITH. Although most who supported fundamentalism in the 1920s still remained in their denominations, many Baptist dispensationalists and a few influential Presbyterians were demanding separatism" (Marsden, *Reforming Fundamentalism: Fuller Seminary and the New Evangelicalism,* Grand Rapids: Eerdmans, 1987, p. 7).

George Dollar, one of the few historians of the Fundamentalist movement to write from the standpoint of a genuine Fundamentalist, gives this definition: "Historic fundamentalism is the literal interpretation of all the affirmations and attitudes of the Bible and the militant exposure of all non-biblical affirmations and attitudes" (Dollar, *A History of Fundamentalism in America,* 1973).

Dollar divides Fundamentalism into three periods. From 1875-1900 conservative leaders raised the banner against Modernism within the denominations. From 1900-1935 these struggles resulted in men leaving their denominations to form separate churches and groups. "They were the architects of ecclesiastical separation." From 1935-1983 the second generation Fundamentalists continued the battle from outside of the mainline denominations and also contended against the New Evangelical movement. It is plain that this historian, who gave a significant portion of his life to the examination of these matters, identifies historic Fundamentalism with earnest militancy and biblical separation.

David O. Beale, who also has written a history of Fundamentalism from a Fundamentalist perspective, gives this definition: "The essence of Fundamentalism ... is the unqualified acceptance of and obedience to the

Scriptures. ... The present study reveals that pre-1930 Fundamentalism was nonconformist, while post-1930 Fundamentalism has been separatist" (Beale, *In Pursuit of Purity: American Fundamentalism Since 1850,* Bob Jones University Press, 1986, p. 5).

I offer one more illustration of the definition given to Fundamentalism by its historians. John Ashbrook has deep roots in the Fundamentalist movement. His father, William, was brought to trial by the Presbyterian denomination because of his stand against Modernism. After his separation from Presbyterianism, William Ashbrook established an independent Fundamentalist church. He wrote an incisive book on New Evangelicalism entitled *Evangelicalism: The New Neutralism*. The first edition of this work appeared in 1958. His son, John, after a period of toying with New Evangelicalism as a young man, became a solid Fundamentalist leader in his own right. His book *New Neutralism II: Exposing the Gray of Compromise* is, in this author's opinion, one of the best books in print on this subject. In looking back over the Fundamentalist movement since the 1930s, John Ashbrook defines Fundamentalism in this way:

> "Fundamentalism is the militant belief and proclamation of the basic doctrines of Christianity leading to a Scriptural separation from those who reject them" (Ashbrook, *Axioms of Separation*, nd., p. 10).

Those who deny the militancy and separation of historic Fundamentalism are trying to rewrite history. Instead of admitting that they have repudiated biblical Fundamentalism and have compromised the Word of God and adopted New Evangelicalism, these revisionists are trying to redefine Fundamentalism to fit their backslidden condition.

2. THAT HISTORIC FUNDAMENTALISM WAS MORE THAN THE AFFIRMATION OF "THE FIVE FUNDAMENTALS" IS PROVEN BY THE FACT OF NEW EVANGELICALISM.

If it were true that historical Fundamentalism was merely a stand for "the five fundamentals," the New Evangelical movement of the 1940s would have made no sense, because New Evangelicalism has always held to "the five fundamentals." In fact, Harold Ockenga, one of the fathers of New Evangelicalism, said that there at least several dozen fundamentals!

It was not a stand for "the five fundamentals" that New Evangelicals protested. The keynote of New Evangelicalism was the repudiation of the separatism and other militant aspects of old-line Fundamentalism, which proves that old-line Fundamentalism was characterized by these things.

In his history of Fuller Theological Seminary, *Reforming Fundamentalism*, historian George M. Marsden makes it plain that Fuller's early leaders were consciously rejecting the negative aspects of old-line Fundamentalism. The title of Marsden's book itself is evidence of the militant character of historic Fundamentalism.

It is clear to honest historians that Fundamentalism fifty years ago was characterized by MILITANCY, by a willingness to deal with the NEGATIVES, and by SEPARATION, and it was this fact that produced the New Evangelical reaction against Fundamentalism.

3. THAT HISTORIC FUNDAMENTALISM WAS MORE THAN THE AFFIRMATION OF "THE FIVE FUNDAMENTALS" IS ACKNOWLEDGED BY

HISTORIC FUNDAMENTALIST ORGANIZATIONS AND PUBLICATIONS.

Consider *The Fundamentalist*, published by J. Frank Norris, an influential fundamental Baptist leader of Texas. Independent Baptist historian George Dollar describes Norris's *The Fundamentalist* in this way:

> "*The Fundamentalist* alarmed and alerted ... Reading the 1920-1930 back issues of *The Fundamentalist*, one can almost see the smoke and hear the battle cries of those times" (Dollar, *The Fight for Fundamentalism*, published by the author, 1983, p. 3).

Norris's paper is representative of that entire generation of Fundamentalism in that it was a generation noted for its bold militancy for the truth.

Consider the following definition of Fundamentalism that was given by the World Congress of Fundamentalists, meeting in 1976 in Usher Hall, Edinburgh, Scotland:

> A Fundamentalist is a born-again believer in the Lord Jesus Christ who--
>
> 1. Maintains an immovable allegiance to the inerrant, infallible, and verbally inspired Bible.
>
> 2. Believes that whatever the Bible says is so.
>
> 3. Judges all things by the Bible and is judged only by the Bible.
>
> 4. Affirms the foundational truths of the historic Christian Faith: The doctrine of the Trinity; the incarnation, virgin birth, substitutionary atonement, bodily resurrection and glorious ascension, and Second Coming of the Lord Jesus Christ; the new birth through regeneration by the Holy Spirit; the resurrection of the saints to life eternal; the resurrection of the ungodly to final judgment and eternal death; the fellowship of the saints, who are the body of Christ.

5. Practices fidelity to that Faith and endeavors to preach it to every creature.

6. Exposes and separates from all ecclesiastical denial of that Faith, compromise with error, and apostasy from the Truth.

7. Earnestly contends for the Faith once delivered.

The Congress summarized its definition in this way: "Fundamentalism is militant orthodoxy set on fire with soulwinning zeal."

Conclusion

As we noted at the beginning of this study, many varying definitions of Fundamentalism have been given through the years, and the truth of the matter is that Fundamentalism has taken a great variety of forms. As a movement, it has been largely interdenominational, yet many independent churches, such as independent Baptists and independent Bible churches, have accepted the label. Regardless of this variety, though, one of the chief hallmarks of Fundamentalism--its very essence, if you will--has always been a MILITANCY for the Faith of the Word of God. Anyone who is not truly militant in standing for the Truth has no right to the title of biblical Fundamentalism.

We close with the words of G. Archer Weniger, who showed the fallacy of the view that Fundamentalism is merely a concern for "the five fundamentals"--

> "The five fundamentals have only to do with the Presbyterian aspect of the struggle with modernism. ... The bulk of Fundamentalism, especially the Baptists of every stripe who composed the majority by far, never accepted the five fundamentals alone. The World's Christian Fundamentals Association, founded in 1919, had

at least a dozen main doctrines highlighted. The same was true of the Fundamental Baptist Fellowship, which originated in 1920. A true Fundamentalist would under no circumstances restrict his doctrinal position to five fundamentals. Even Dr. Carl F.H. Henry, a New Evangelical theologian, listed at least several dozen doctrines essential to the Faith. The only advantage of reducing the Faith down to five is to make possible a wider inclusion of religionists, who might be way off in heresy on other specific doctrines. It is much easier to have large numbers of adherents with the lowest common denominator in doctrine" (G. Archer Weniger, quoted in *Calvary Contender*, April 15, 1994).

WE SHOULD LIMIT OUR MESSAGE TO BROADEN OUR FELLOWSHIP

The following important challenge is by Pastor David Nettleton and is published by the General Association of Regular Baptist Churches --

> "I am pure from the blood of all men. For I have not shunned to declare unto you all the counsel of God." Acts 20:27

This message, like many, is born out of an experience. It may be some others are going through similar experiences. Therefore, let me recount the one which brought this message to light.

I was brought up as a Presbyterian. I was saved at a college which was interdenominational in student body, but was managed by the Church of the Brethren. From there I went to a seminary which was not a denominational school, and from there to another seminary which was United Presbyterian. I entered the Baptist pastorate with no Baptist training except that which came from reading of the Scriptures.

A few years later I was drawn into an interdenominational youth movement and was given the leadership of a local Saturday night rally. I cooperated with any who were evangelical, regardless of their associations. I was advised by top leaders in the movement to seek the names of outstanding modernists for my advisory committee. I didn't do that. But I did follow advice which led me to send to all converts back to the churches of their choice, churches I knew to be liberal in some cases. This greatly troubled my conscience and I prayed and thought about it.

Another problem connected with this work was the failure on my part to instruct any converts on the matter of Christian baptism, which in the Scriptures is the first test of obedience. I felt that I should do this inasmuch as Peter and Paul did it. But how could it be done when on the committee of the work there were close friends who did not believe it? By such an association I had definitely stripped my message and my ministry of important Bible truths which many called "nonessentials."

In the follow-up work it was not convenient to speak of eternal security in the presence of Christian workers who hated the name of the doctrine. Thus the ministry was pared down to the gospel, just as if there was nothing in the Great Commission about baptizing converts and indoctrinating them. I had found the least common denominator and I was staying by it. But my conscience had no rest. Then it was that Acts 20:27 came to mean something to me.

The great apostle had never allowed himself to be drawn into anything which would limit his message. He could say with a clean conscience, "I am pure from the blood of all men. For I have not shunned to declare unto you all the counsel of God." Why cannot many say that today? In my case, and in many other cases, it was due to a desire to teach a larger audience and to work with a larger group of Christians. Many have been carried away from full obedience by a noble-sounding motto which has been applied to Christian work. "In essentials unity, in nonessentials liberty, and in all things charity." Some things are not essential to salvation but they are essential to full obedience, and the Christian has no liberty under God to sort out the

Scriptures into essentials and nonessentials! It is our duty to declare the whole counsel of God, and to do it wherever we are.

Paul had a wonderfully balanced ministry. In his preaching he would never please men, for he knew he could not be pleasing to God if he tried to please men. Yet in his living he testified, "I am made all things to all men, that I might by all means save some" (1 Cor. 9:22). "Even as I please all men in all things, not seeking mine own profit, but the profit of many, that they may be saved" (1 Cor. 10:33). What a happy balance this is in the ministry! It is true, humble, and wholesome.

Today we are choosing between two alternatives. A LIMITED MESSAGE OR A LIMITED FELLOWSHIP. If we preach all of the Bible truths, there are many places where we will never be invited. If we join hands with the crowds, there will be limiting of the message of the Bible. Bear this in mind--it is the Baptist who lays aside the most! It is the fundamental Baptist who makes the concessions! Think this through and you will find it to be true. We believe in believer's baptism. We believe in separation. We preach eternal security. We believe in the imminent coming of Christ. We consider it an act of obedience to reprove unbelief in religious circles. The Sadduccee and the Pharisee are to be labeled. But according to a present philosophy we must lay these things aside for the sake of a larger sphere of service.

Which is more important, full obedience or a larger sphere of service? And yet I do not fully believe these are the only two alternatives. It is our first duty to be fully obedient to God in all things, and then to wait upon Him for the places of service. It may be that we will be limited, and it may be that we will not. Charles Haddon Spurgeon did not travel as widely as some men of his day, but his sermons have traveled as far as the sermons of most men.

I have recently read a religious article by a great evangelist. He deplores the moral conditions in America. He deplores the conditions in our schools. He speaks against the liquor traffic and against juvenile delinquency. But nothing is said against America's greatest enemy--THE MODERN BELIEF WHICH GOES FORTH FROM SUPPOSEDLY CHRISTIAN CHURCHES. The strength of the nation lies in her love of God. That love has grown cold in many churches, and Jesus Christ our Lord is called an illegitimate child, a confused young man and a dead teacher. That kind of thing needs to be rebuked at the cost of reputation and even at the cost of life, if need be. But as soon as it is rebuked, the man who rebukes it will lose the majority of his following, if he is gaining that following through cooperation with modernistic churches.

It is my belief that some of our great evangelists today are thorough Bible-believing Christians. They accept nearly every truth in the Book. It seems they refrain from preaching all the counsel of God for one reason. To them, it is important to reach farther even if we reach with a smaller message. The breach within so-called Protestantism today is as great as the breach between Protestantism and Roman Catholicism. We need to make this fact known. But every time we promote the inclusive type of ministry we are covering up a fact that needs to be known.

God has given us a great message to preach. It

contains the glorious gospel of our Lord Jesus Christ, but it is not limited to that gospel. He has commissioned us to preach the gospel, baptize our converts and indoctrinate them (Matt. 28:19-20). He has given us the very best system of follow-up work, which is the building of Bible-believing churches and joining converts to them. He is calling us to loyalty and obedience.

We need no new message. We need no new method. We need only the spirit of obedience found in Paul when he testified, *"For I have not shunned to declare unto you all the counsel of God."*

WE SHOULD BE BALANCED

Through the years I have been challenged many times to be more "balanced." Recently I asked preachers to write and let me know if they are edified by this ministry. More than 200 replied in a matter of days and most were overwhelmingly positive. Three or four said that though they appreciated the material, they wished I was a little more "balanced." What does this mean? I have been meditating and praying about this matter, and the following thoughts came to mind:

1. BALANCE MEANS PREACHING THE WHOLE COUNSEL OF GOD.

Paul reminded the Ephesian elders that he had declared to them *"all the counsel of God"* (Acts 20:27). This is the job of every preacher, but particularly of a pastor or a church planter. Every part of the Bible, every doctrine, is important. No preacher has the liberty to say "I will preach some doctrines, but the rest I am not responsible for," or "I will just preach the Gospel," or "I will just focus on this or that topic (the family, creation science, Bible versions, separation, etc.) and not concern myself with other things."

Since God first called me to preach, I have always been convinced of the importance of preaching and contending for the whole counsel of God. For our church planting ministry in South Asia I have developed a Bible school curriculum to train preachers. We train them in the whole counsel of God. After 20 years of studying and teaching the whole counsel of God, I completed the *Way of Life Encyclopedia of the Bible & Christianity*, which deals with every doctrine of the Scripture. The book *Things Hard to Be Understood*, which we published in 1997, also seeks to deal with everything in the Word of God, including the most difficult parts.

If balance means preaching the whole counsel of God, I am balanced.

Careful readers will note that even via the Fundamental Baptist Information Service we deal with a very wide variety of doctrines and issues. The current event items are not selected haphazardly. We do not emulate the Religious News Service or the Ecumenical News Service in attempting to cover every major current event in "Christendom" or in the ecumenical or denominational world. One of our chief goals is to select events that illustrate doctrinal truths which are being attacked. We do not merely report on events and personalities and books and speeches. We analyze these with the Word of God and sound doctrine. We deal with the Gospel, justification, the church, sanctification, prophecy, Christian living, biblical inspiration and preservation, and countless other aspects of biblical truth. We focus on the things that we feel are at the forefront of the devil's attack upon the truth and upon New Testament churches today.

2. BALANCE MEANS FULFILLING THE GREAT COMMISSION.

The term Great Commission is not in the Scripture, but there was a "great commission" given by the risen Lord Jesus Christ to the apostles and through them to the churches. It is emphasized by the Holy Spirit in that it is repeated five times (Matthew 24; Mark 16; Luke 24; John 20; Acts 1). This commission is to preach the gospel to every creature and every nation, to baptize and disciple those who believe, and ultimately to establish sound New Testament congregations wherever the Word of God is spread. This commission is to be perpetuated until Christ returns. It is the general marching orders for the churches. We see the Great Commission fulfilled and exemplified in the lives of the apostles. They did not turn aside to political activity or to establish social movements. They gave themselves exclusively to the preaching of the gospel and the founding of churches that would perpetuate this Commission. Every God-called preacher is under obligation to give himself to the fulfillment of the Great Commission.

There is a "balance" defined for us here. Every preacher is to be busy preaching the gospel. Every preacher is to be busy discipling converts. Every preacher is to be involved in the establishment of strong churches. This does not mean that a man will not be focused more or less on certain parts of the Commission. Gifts and calling are different. Philip the evangelist focused on the preaching of the gospel (Acts 8:5-40), while Barnabas focused on the establishment of the new disciples (Acts 11:19-26), but this is not to say that Barnabas did not preach the gospel to the unsaved or that Philip did not disciple Christians. No preacher can say that God has not called him to evangelize the lost or that God has not called him to disciple the saved. No preacher has the authority to ignore the New Testament church and go about evangelizing or discipling apart from the church. To be "balanced" means the preacher is seeking to do the whole work of the Great Commission.

If all I did was write articles for the Fundamental Baptist Information Service, and I did not seek to take the gospel to the unsaved and to disciple Christians and to be a fruitful member of a New Testament church, I would not be balanced. I do all of these things, though, and I always have. Obviously the Fundamental Baptist Information Service and *O Timothy* magazine take much of my time, but they are only two of the things I do. I believe this is what has kept me on a very practical level in my writings. Theorizing and "theologizing" doesn't interest me, because it doesn't help anyone in a practical sense. I want to preach something that will help people. Preaching the Word of God for many years in one of the world's poorest countries and in county jails tends to keep one's feet on the ground.

3. BALANCE MEANS FULFILLING ALL THE RESPONSIBILITIES OF THE CHRISTIAN LIFE.

> "Having therefore these promises, dearly beloved, let us cleanse ourselves from ALL filthiness of the flesh and spirit, perfecting holiness in the fear of God" (2 Cor. 7:1).
>
> "For ye were sometimes darkness, but now are ye light in the Lord: walk as children of light: (For the fruit of the Spirit is in ALL goodness and righteousness and truth" (Eph. 5:7-8).
>
> "But as he which hath called you is holy, so be ye holy in ALL manner of conversation" (1 Peter 1:15).
>
> "Now I praise you, brethren, that ye remember me in ALL things, and keep the ordinances, as I delivered them to you" (1 Cor. 11:2).

Notice the "all" in each of the previous verses. Balance, therefore, would surely involve obedience to every duty God has laid out for us in the New Testament Scriptures. That is a tall order! It means seeking to be pure in thought and deed and speech, walking in the light, confessing one's sins. It means being a good father, a good mother, an obedient child. It means loving the brethren, being patient with the weak, submitting to governmental authorities, praying for all men. It means being a dedicated and fruitful church member, preaching the gospel to every creature, earnestly contending for the faith. It means keeping oneself unspotted from the world. The list is as long as the New Testament faith. Is any Christian really "balanced" in fulfilling all of the responsibilities of the Christian life? Not by a long shot, but that must be our goal.

4. BALANCE DEPENDS ON A MAN'S GIFT AND CALLING.

A survey of the Bible reveals that God calls different men to different things and he gifts them differently. That is true in the New Testament churches. There are a number of gifts and callings described in Romans 12; 1 Corinthians 12; Ephesians 4; 1 Timothy 3; and 1 Peter 4. A pastor's gift and calling and focus will not be exactly the same as that of an evangelist or a prophet or a missionary church planter. We don't believe there are prophets in the churches today in the same sense as in the apostolic times; there is no revelation being given today; but there is a prophetic gift still given in the sense of applying the Word of God to these present times. The term "prophecy" is used in a very general sense in 1 Cor. 14:3, "But he that prophesieth speaketh unto men to edification, and exhortation, and comfort."

The point here, though, is not to define the various

gifts and callings, but merely to note the fact that there are differences in them. Certainly this gets at the heart of the mysterious and allusive matter of "balance." A "balanced" ministry for an evangelist is not the same as a "balanced" ministry for a pastor or church planter, etc. Even among pastors or elders there are significant differences in gifts and personalities and vision and many other things that result in great differences in "balance."

My calling has always been along what I consider to be the prophetic, meaning the application of the Word of God to these times, of discerning the apostasy of these last hours, of calling God's people to repentance, of understanding the broad scope and the end result of various movements rather than merely the narrow focus of what these are actually attempting to accomplish today.

During our early years as missionary church planters in South Asia, I entered unwittingly into an intensive firsthand course in end-times apostasy and ecumenism by my experiences with various "Christian" groups and movements and churches in that part of the world. To my knowledge we were the only fundamentalist type missionaries in all of Nepal. There was no like-minded fellowship for hundreds of miles. We did the best we could to get along with the various ecumenical organizations and churches that were there, but it was difficult, both for us and for them! A group of ecumenical Christian leaders, including the head of Campus Crusade for Christ and the head of the Nepal Bible Society, eventually held something like an ecclesiastical trial, brought charges of divisiveness to the "body of Christ in Nepal" against me, and demanded that we "stop all ministry" and "leave the country as soon as possible." We didn't leave, but you can see that things were not going smoothly between us and the ecumenical brethren! I learned a lot from those amazing experiences. (Bear with me; I am moving toward my point.)

When I first began publishing *O Timothy* magazine in 1984, I traveled to Serampore University (founded by the famous Baptist missionary William Carey) near Calcutta, India, and recorded an interview with the head of the seminary. The man was also a professor of New Testament theology. He told me that there are a number of ways to become a Christian--be baptized, be born into a Christian home, etc. The one way he did NOT mention was to be born again through faith in the finished atonement of Jesus Christ. He told me that he believed Hindus and Buddhists would go to heaven if they were sincere in their own faith. Soon after this, I published the interview in *O Timothy* magazine (it can be found in the *O Timothy Computer Library* under the issues for the year 1984). The man wrote me an angry letter, rebuking me for printing this. I had explained to him exactly who I was and why I wanted to interview him, and he had allowed the tape recorded interview; yet he was upset when his own words appeared in print. I learned through this and other experiences during those days that it is common for false teachers and compromisers to attempt to hide things, to be less than forthright about their doctrinal positions, to believe and do things in their ministries that are not reported to their supporters, etc. I learned that in order to know the truth about many things in "Christianity" one has to dig for the facts, that the truth is not always out in the open.

As I was reading my Bible in those days I came upon the passage in Ezekiel 8:5-18, in which Ezekiel was instructed to dig into the wall of the temple to observe things that were being done in secret by the apostate religious leaders of his day. I felt that this is exactly what God wanted me to do in my day. I had to "dig into the wall" and observe the false and wicked things of apostate Christianity and rebuke those things with God's Word and report them to God's people to protect them from error and duplicity. I had to read their writings and interview them and analyze them and find out the truth of what they really believe and practice. This is part of my calling. It is certainly not pleasant; it is not something very many men should do; but it is essential for the protection of the churches just as in Ezekiel's day it was important that the prophet know what was happening in the secret places of the apostasy.

At that time I started a section in *O Timothy* called "Digging in the Walls" which continues to this day. And the Fundamental Baptist Information Service is partly the "Digging in the Walls" section of *O Timothy* magazine in a daily electronic format. This is a large part of my focus and calling. That does not mean that I ignore the whole counsel of God; it simply means that my focus is different than that of some other God-called men.

If a pastor preached only the type of things that I publish in "Digging in the Walls," he would be unbalanced. But for me to preach like that and focus on that type of thing, because God has called and gifted me to do so, is not an imbalance. To think it is, is to fail to understand that there are different gifts and callings.

5. BALANCE DEPENDS ON THE CIRCUMSTANCE.

Finally, balance has a lot to do with the particular circumstance in which a preacher finds himself. Noah "preached righteousness" for 120 years as the ark was being constructed. Was Noah balanced? The people who heard him preach probably didn't think so. He was too negative. Jeremiah was constantly negative toward Israel. Was Jeremiah balanced? Sure he was. He was preaching exactly what God told him to preach, and he was preaching exactly what apostate, backsliding Israel needed to hear. What about Amos or Jonah? What about John the Baptist? He lived out in the wilderness and preached repentance, repentance, repentance. Was he balanced? Not by man's standards, but he was balanced by God's. He was preaching exactly what God told him to preach and he was preaching exactly what his hearers needed to hear.

The circumstance will somewhat determine the "balance" of a man's ministry. You see this in the New Testament epistles. The message given to the churches depended upon their condition at that particular time. If a church is becoming worldly and carnal and is in a moral tailspin, should a preacher ignore this and preach about something else? By no means! The condition of his people will largely determine what he needs to preach and what he needs to be doing.

Am I "balanced"? Are you, fellow preachers, "balanced"? There is only one absolute measure for that. The measure is not whether your "negative" preaching is balanced by an equal amount of "positive" preaching. The measure is not what some other preachers are doing or what some group of people think about my ministry. The measure is not New Evangelical church growth principles. The measure is not some man's idea of what the church's purpose should be. The measure is the Holy Scriptures and the perfect will of God for me and my life and ministry. Only the Holy Spirit can guide a man in the "balance" for his life and ministry.

Be balanced, brethren!